Partible Paternity and Anthropological Theory

The Construction of an Ethnographic Fantasy

Warren Shapiro

UNIVERSITY PRESS OF AMERICA,® INC.

Lanham • Boulder • New York • Toronto • Plymouth, UK

Copyright © 2009 by
University Press of America,® Inc.
4501 Forbes Boulevard
Suite 200
Lanham, Maryland 20706
UPA Acquisitions Department (301) 459-3366

Estover Road
Plymouth PL6 7PY
United Kingdom

Library of Congress Control Number: 2009922981
ISBN: 978-0-7618-4532-4 (paperback : alk. paper)
eISBN: 978-0-7618-4533-1

Most (cultural) anthropologists reject the basic concepts of sociobiology . . . and have turned their backs on sociobiologists rather than involve them in serious discussion. This seems a strategic mistake . . . (Peletz 1995, 366)

Contents

List of Tables   vii

Acknowledgments   ix

Introduction   1

1   Three Primitivist Projects   3

2   The Grand Claims of Beckerman and Valentine   11

3   The Northwest Amazon Cases   23

4   Other Pertinent Cases: General Considerations   31

5   Evidence Re Focality in Kin Classification *Simpliciter*   33

6   Evidence Re Focality in Kin Classification Stemming from Partible Paternity   37

7   Evidence Re the Residential and Symbolic Isolation of the Sexually Bonded Pair and Dependent Offspring   41

8   Evidence Re Sexual Jealousy   45

9   Evidence Re the Denigration of Women   47

10 Miscellaneous Evidence   51

11 Conclusion   55

Bibliography   57

List of Tables

Table 3.1.   My Tabulation
Table 4.1.   Names and Locations of Amazonian Populations with Partible
             Paternity Outside the Northwest Amazon

Acknowledgments

Portions of this book were read at a kinship symposium in Memory of Per Hage at the American Anthropological Association meetings in 2006. I am greatly indebted to the following individuals who have worked in Amazonia for unpublished information they supplied to me via email: Bob Carneiro, Janet Chernela, Lori Cormier, Bill Crocker, Bill Fisher, Tom Gregor, Kim Hill, Waud Kracke, Laura Rival, Tony Seeger, Janet Siskind, Allie Stearman, Terry Turner, and Aparecida Vilaça. Tom Gregor needs to be singled for his very considerable encouragement as well. Hal Scheffler provided his usual thorough and penetrating review of the original manuscript. Others who read and commented on it include Herbert Bell, Vicky Burbank, Herb Damsky, Bev Gaglione, Ward Goodenough, Brian Kinstler, Tom Parides, Laura Rival, Mel Spiro, Melvin Stanger, and George Will. My niece, Lisa Lauer, who has far greater computer skills than I, did the final typing of the manuscript.

Introduction

This short book continues my examination of primitivist thought among both anthropologists and the people they study (W. Shapiro 1990, 1996, 1998, 2005). Like its predecessors, it deals with particular empirical problems—in this case (1) what has been called "partible paternity"—or "multiple paternity" (Carneiro n.d.), or "plural paternity" (Cormier 2003, 64–65), or "co-paternity" (Kensinger 2002), or "polyandrous conception'" (Erickson 2002), or "male co-procreation" (Àles 2002)—the ideology, especially common in Amazonia, that several sexual acts are necessary to create and sustain a fetus, and that the mother may have these with more than one man; and (2) a recent analysis of this phenomenon by Beckerman and Valentine (2002b). I argue that the latter is remarkably (if unintentionally) akin to Morgan's fantasies (1877) about an "early" human condition of "group marriage," subsequently taken up by Engels (1884) and now one of the staples of primitivist thought, and that partible paternity itself is more realistically analyzed trough a combination of evolutionary psychology—an intellectual heir of sociobiology—and cognitive science, on which, *pace* Peletz in my epigraph, most cultural anthropologists have also turned their backs. But first I need to situate and address all this back-turning, for so many turned backs betoken so many closed minds, and this is not something of which a discipline born of the Enlightenment can be proud—or, indeed, should tolerate.

1

Chapter One

Three Primitivist Projects

I consider here three examples of primitivist thinking in contemporary anthropology—either expressly primitivist or implicitly so, insofar as ethnographic materials from the Fourth World are employed in the service of critiques of what is construed as "Western Civilization" and especially of "Western" science. The critiques are remarkably uninformed, insofar as they evidence little or nothing beyond a layperson's knowledge of what people in the Darwinian disciplines actually do—what Daly and Wilson (1988, 152–156) call "biophobia." The expression is apt because it suggests a fear-driven attitude towards something, which is therefore avoided and/or treated with denigration rather than rational confrontation. Thus:

(1) *Primitive communism exists in the Fourth World and is somehow "inherent" in the human condition*. This is, of course, vintage Engels, and it implies not only communization of productive property but, as well, unstructured sharing, the familization of sociality, collective mating ("group marriage"), and hence the absence of sexual jealousy and, related, the presence of gender equality. Most of this cluster of characteristics is examined against the Amazonian materials in the body of the present book. Here I want to focus on Richard Lee's career-long flirtation with "primitive communism," especially with reference to his !Kung Bushman data.

Although even in *Man the Hunter* (Lee and DeVore 1968) there are hints of this embrace, it has emerged as a full-blown romance only in more recent years. Thus, at one of the successors to the Man the Hunter conference, Lee declared that

> historical materialism argues that there exists a core of culture in primitive society that is intimately linked to mode of production. It is much longer-lived, has a much deeper time-depth, than Western capitalist culture . . . [T]his culture core

is communist: it embraces the collective right to basic resources and an egalitarian political order . . . [O]ur ancestors were communists (Lee 1988, 255).

Taking these remarks to be empirical statements testable by appeal to the ethnographic data on the !Kung and other hunter-gatherers, I think three is some reason for skepticism. I am satisfied that the hunter-gatherers in general exhibit "the collective right to basic resources," though I would add that this has at least as much to do with remarkably low population densities as with a communitarian spirit *simpliciter*. For the latter is just not there, not in the unalloyed form Lee suggests, not even for the !Kung. Thus, the !Kung homicide rate exceeds that of the United States (Konner 1990, 162–63); !Kung social classification draws a distinction between kin and non-kin, despite the fact that kin-terms are universally applied (Marshall 1976, 214); !Kung notions of reciprocity towards non-kin depend heavily upon coercion (*ibid.,* 298 *et seq.*)—what has been called "demand sharing" (Peterson 1997); and among the !Kung, close consanguineal or affinal kinship is crucial in residential choice (Marshall 1976, 182) and other areas of behavior. And consider this from Marshall (1976, 288): "Altruism, kindness, sympathy, or genuine generosity were not qualities that I observed often in their behavior. However, these qualities were not entirely lacking, *especially between parents and offspring, between siblings, and between spouses*" (emphasis added). Finally, !Kung women are consigned, voluntarily or no, to those archdemons of Marxist theology, nuclear families (*ibid*, 254); they are barred from having anything to do with ritual fire (*ibid.,* 83) and may not touch oracular implements (*ibid.,* 153); and they are subjected to polygyny, usually against their will (*ibid.,* 262–265).[1]

The case for "primitive communism" among the !Kung is thus exceedingly weak. But this is an empirical conclusion, and I am not at all sure that Lee's paean to historical materialism, quoted above, is derived, however indirectly, from anything observable in the external world. Indeed, the evocation of time-depth and ancestry, as I have argued elsewhere (W. Shapiro 1998), is, in the absence of anything like a fossil record, entirely metaphorical. In the manner of origin myths elsewhere, imageries of temporal and spatial depth ("a *core* of culture") are employed to mask a personal sense of ontological and moral priority. This is nothing if not classical primitivism. The point is especially worth making, I think, because it suggests how essentialist imagery can be fabricated even with a blatant hostility towards—and an apparent ignorance of—current research in the Darwinian disciplines. For example, Lee and Daly (1987, 30) observe that male domination of women is "a historical and cultural question" and not "a question of biology, innateness, and universality." This notion of "innateness" signals the innate/learned dichotomy of popular imagination, something Darwinian scholars have abandoned for just about four decades (Lehrman 1970). Equally archaic is the idea that genetic codes invariably—"universally"—result in a particular behavior: so far as I am aware, everyone working in evolutionary psychology employs probability calculi (Pinker 2002, 122). These misconstructions are especially remarkable because Lee has persistently represented himself as committed to scientific paradigms (see esp. Lee 1992). Yet alongside his impressive corpus of data on !Kung nutrition, land use, and other solid subjects (Lee 1968, 1979) dwells a Marxist metaphysician.

(2) *Women have no genetic inclination towards maternal behavior, which stems instead from a series of local constructions.* If this were true, it would mean that human females are unique among sexually reproducing species in having reproductively significant internal anatomy and physiology, but not corresponding behavioral and emotional propensities absent external—and particular—instruction. This is, of course, a common position—dogmatically held—in feminist circles, one brought into mainstream anthropology by Scheper-Hughes (1992). A more recent example can be found in Alma Gottlieb's study of childcare among the Beng of the Ivory Coast. Her words:

> [T]here are serious problems with the popular assumption of a maternal instinct. . . . First and most obviously, not all women intentionally become mothers. For those who deliberately eschew motherhood, how relevant is the postulated maternal instinct? In other words, if maternity is such a strong instinct, why would some women opt to avoid it, and how might individual women manage to overcome the presumed urge? . . . On a different note, what do we make of abusive mothers—women who behave violently or neglectfully toward their own children in ways that decidedly fall outside the scope of that hypothesized gentle instinct? . . . (Gottlieb 2004, 50–51).

The terms "instinct" and "urge," I think, are unfortunate ones, insofar as they suggest a *deus et machina*, an agent within the agent an individual feels to be himself/herself. Although people working in the Darwinian disciplines still frequently evoke such imagery (Oyama 1985), it signals supernatural agency and is thus outside the bailiwick of empirical research. It also recalls the obsolete innate/learned dichotomy. Note again the mistaken idea that a Darwinian perspective requires universality. From this standpoint, abusive and neglectful motherhood, and the eschewing of motherhood altogether, though certainly worthy of attention and explanation, are not especially salient issues. Far more compelling are the cross-cultural data indicating that, apparently everywhere, most women play maternal roles (Whiting and Edwards 1988); that they relinquish such roles when they are unable to care for children and even then with some ambivalence (Scheper-Hughes 1992; Silk

1987); that communal projects for early childcare have an established track record of gross failure (Brumann 2000; Tiger and Shepher 1975) largely because women, in defiance of local constructions, insist on nurturing their own children; that women as contrasted with men tend to have certain characteristics that make them better at handling infants, such as higher and less threatening voices, a greater ability for sustained eye-contact, a greater tendency to smile, and a generally greater comfort with intimacy and discomfort with aloofness (Dabbs 2000); and that the vast majority of people who have carried out research on childcare, like Scheper-Hughes and Gottlieb, are women.

(3) *There are not two gender-classes but three.* Or more, according to some. This claim—like the denial of maternal "instinct" and the assertion of "primitive communism"—has become heavily politicized, with the victim classes here being neither women nor "tribal" people *per se*, but those who advertise themselves as "gender-benders." Yet in fine primitivist tradition, the alleged evidence comes mostly from the Fourth World, especially from a cluster of Native American institutions known to a more innocent generation as "berdache",[2] and the critique opposes these "tribal" understandings with the alleged parochialism of "Western" notions of gender, which nowadays are assigned the pejorative labels "heterocentric" or "heteronormative." Also warranting emphasis is the logical connection between "third sex" theory and the "radical" feminist assertion that sex and gender are entirely separate matters.

A particularly instructive and well-studied case is the Navaho status rendered as *nadle* or as some phonetic variation thereof. The term itself has been variously translated as "being transformed" (Hill 1935, 273), "one who changes continuously" (W. Roscoe 1994, 356), and "hermaphrodite" (Epple 1997, 175). This last rendition is especially revealing, though the liminal position of the *nadle* is implied by the other two. The native term thus refers not to a third *focal* or central gender class, on a logical par with "male" and "female," but to a nonfocal category which is *logically dependent upon* these last two classes. Moreover, Hill (1935, 273) notes that *only* hermaphrodites are "real" members of the *nadle* class, whereas biological males or females who attempt to effect this position by cross-dressing are rendered by an expression translatable as "those who pretend to be *nadle*." In other words, this liminal category is itself subject to a focal/nonfocal distinction, with focality being dependent upon anatomical characteristics.[3] As Lang (1998, 141) puts it in her masterful summary of the "berdache" date: "Among the Navajo, aspects of physical intersexuality became fixed points in relation to which non-intersexuals—'those who pretend to be *nadle*'—had to orient themselves." This is anything but a challenge to "Western" understandings.

Also pertinent here is the current preference for the appellation "two-spirit person" over "berdache." Pilling (1997, 69) puts it succinctly: "two-spirit" refers to persons who are a blend of the feminine and the masculine, the woman and the man." This is usually echoed in native lexicons, where "two-spirit people" are designated by expressions which translate into "womanly man" and "manly woman" (Lang 1997, 103, 1998, 247–51; see also Thayer 1980).

Despite these data, the illusion of a "third sex" persists. Thus, Herdt (1994, 21) writes of "the limitations of a reproductive paradigm" in studies of gender classification.[4] Cromwell (1997, 133) speaks disparagingly of the "myth of only two genders" but in the same paragraph indicts "the medico-psychological establishment's refusal to acknowledge individuals who maintain *an intermediate status* (emphasis added). And this establishment, according to Evelyn Blackwood, is in collusion with "Western" folk theory. Her words:

> Dominant gender ideology in America equates one's sex with one's gender. Most non-Native Americans have difficulty perceiving a physical male as a woman or a physical female as a man. The critical importance of biology to Western constructs of gender meant that white scholars were rarely able to separate biology from gender successfully when talking about two-spirit people. Most non-Native scholars referred to two-spirits by the pronoun appropriate to physical sex, not gender. . . . These terms give undue emphasis to the biological aspect of a two-spirit person and tend to overshadow the importance of their social being (Blackwood 1997, 285).

There are, of course, familiar "postmodern" themes here—the charge of "Western" ideological hegemony ("Dominant gender ideology") and parochialism (". . . white scholars were rarely able . . ."), the biology/culture (sex/gender) dichotomy, and the claim of non-Western cosmopolitanism in gender classification—this last supported only by a reassortment of "Western" gender categories. The possibility that these categories are universal, occasionally abetted by further but derived, i.e. nonfocal, categories, seems only occasionally to occur to "third sex" theorists.[5]

Several points, implicit or explicit, in the foregoing considerations should be stressed, for they will come up again in connection with partible paternity. I have already noted the first, viz. the demonization of "the West" that is characteristic of primitivist projects. Another is the minimal attention given to this alleged entity: "the West" is portrayed as a monolith of acquisitiveness or narrowmindedness instead of having multiple perspectives of its own, and of being a particulate creature and not an historical synthesis. The material well-being that only capitalism creates is ignored, as is the progress of science and medicine, the emancipation from State-dominated religion, and the rest of the heritage of skepticism, accountability, and demonstrability known in saner days as the Western European Enlightenment. The focus here is not disinterested comparison, but the promulgation of a Manichean scheme masqueraded as anthropology's "cutting edge."

The opposite side of this scheme—and here is a third point—"tribal" people, women, "gender-benders"—is rendered as having a more acute awareness and a deeper appreciation of things, a Higher Consciousness. This is, of course, standard primitivist melodrama. But there is a fourth point here: because of this Higher Consciousness, the perspectives—the "voices," as one says these days—of these classes must be seen (or heard) in minute detail—"from the native's point of view," in the parlance of today's most illustrious advocate of what Whorf called "incommensurability" (Geertz 1983, 55), nowadays renamed "radical alterity."[6] Never mind that the !Kung and other Fourth World people are anything but "primitive communists," that the majority of the world's women elect to be mothers, and that Native Americans (among others) patently do *not* posit a third focal gender class. Which is to say that the "voices" we are hearing are not so much those of the oppressed as those of an intellectual elite dedicated, supposedly, to their service. I think we have a right to question whether such elites should be allowed to (mis)represent them.

Here is yet a fifth point. The dismissal or underappreciation of science by today's anthropological primitivists is especially noteworthy: Gross and Levitt (1994) have documented this more widely, and in excruciating detail, among academics. It is, of course, consistent with the "biophobia" noted above. It fits too with the remarkable loss of interest by anthropologists in the scientific traditions of the very people they have canonically studied. Whereas earlier generations of scholars respectfully catalogued and attempted to analyze "primitive" systems of knowledge, their "postmodern" successors see only "constructs," related not to the natural world, but (if anything at all) to "power" and "mystification." The Primitive Mind, whose rationality Boas, Lèvi-Strauss, and others so admired, is nowadays seen as something Beyond Rationality, something reflective and intuitive. This is itself mystification, an indication of anthropology's retreat into neoromanticism (Adams 1998, 108–10).

A final point: In addition to (or part of) their hostility to science, anthropology's neoromantics have managed to avoid the issue of focality, that is, again, the possibility that the "constructs" or categories their ethnography reveals have both primary and secondary referents. To take some obvious examples from paternal kinship, the domain to which the body of this essay is devoted, I might use the term "father" in reference to both my genitor and to a Roman Catholic priest but, presumably, it is clear that the former is the primary (focal, real, true) member of his class, whereas the latter's membership is secondary. Also secondary is the membership of individuals whom I might refer to as a *godfather,* a *stepfather,* a *foster father*, and, in the realm of sheer imagery, *Father Time*. Floyd Lounsbury and Harold Scheffler made much the same point as early as 1964 (e.g. Lounsbury 1964, 1969; Scheffler 1978; Scheffler and Lounsbury 1971), but they tended to draw the focal/nonfocal line too starkly (W. Shapiro 2005, 55). Others working in cognitive anthropology and cognitive psychology have corrected this defect in numerous domains (see D'Andrade 1995, 104–21 for an overview), and it is now at least a reasonable conjecture that this is how the human brain creates and organizes categories (see esp. Lakoff 1987). This being so, it is utterly mistaken to regard ethnography which ignores the matter as being "from the native's point of view." It is, on the contrary, a serious misinterpretation of that view.

We are now in a better position to consider Beckerman and Valentine. In what follows, I argue that theirs is a primitivist project and, as such, it exhibits the sort of mystification and self-delusion that can be found in other such projects; and I shall try, in the spirit of the Enlightenment, to get to the truth of the matter.

NOTES

1. This brief enumeration hardly does justice to the extent of !Kung sexism. A fuller treatment is intended for another occasion.

2. This term is considered politically incorrect by some, but others use it freely. I shall follow their lead.

3. See also Witherspoon's analysis of gender in Navaho ontology (1977, 140–43), where only two such classes are posited; and Reichard's report (cited in Lang 1998, 48) that a male who has been emasculated in war was classed as a *nadle*.

4. This, of course, echoes Schneider (1984) on kinship and is approximately as absurd, for much the same reasons (W. Shapiro 2003, 2005). I return to the matter below.

5. My conclusions here are by no means new (see e.g. Besnier 1994; Callender and Kochems 1983, 453; Scheffler 1991, 377–78). Lang (1998) provides considerable information which supports this view, though she seems ambivalent about the matter. Besnier's analysis of the analytical muddles and political flim-flam of the "third sex" theorists is especially penetrating.

6. For a clear statement of Whorf's impact on anthropological epistemology, see Fishman (1960). The definitive critique of today's neo-relativism is Spiro (1986).

Chapter Two

The Grand Claims of Beckerman and Valentine

Beckerman and Valentine hold that partible paternity challenges the "One Sperm, One Fertilization Doctrine" espoused by "Western" science, which, erroneously, relies upon "our common Western view of [single] paternity as universal" (2002b, 3). I shall argue later that partible paternity is considerably less of a challenge to "Western" understandings—popular and scientific— than might be supposed. What I wish to stress now are the implication that these understandings, though correct, are at the same time parochial; and that "Western" science and popular appreciations are in some (unspecified) sort of malignant collusion. We are on ground that is by now surely familiar: the "postmodern" assertion that, in "the West," science and lay knowledge are re- flexes of each other, and the contention, also "postmodern," that empirical ac- curacy is not of any great importance in the evaluation of a theory. Note too the essentialization of both partible paternity and "the West," as if these were particulate entities locked in mortal combat: this of course recalls the melo- dramatic quality characteristic of primitivist projects.

In point of fact, partible paternity may not be as distinct a phenomena as Beckerman and Valentine suppose. Even aside from a long ethnographic record of erroneously assigning a single conception ideology to a community (Conklin 2001b, 147; Loizos and Heady 1999), there are ethnographically known intermediaries between single paternity and partible paternity, as well as certain remarkable permutations of these themes. Thus, the Kawahiv of the Maderia River in Central Brazil have not only partible paternity *in sensu stricto*, but another form of shared paternity, wherein:

> a shaman brings his successor into being by dreaming of a spirit who comes to him and asks to be born; in the dream he directs the spirit to a particular expec- tant woman. The child who is then born to that woman is considered to be the

embodiment of that spirit and is spoken of as the "offspring" . . . of the shaman who dreamed him. With training (usually by the dreaming shaman) the child then becomes a shaman (Waud Kracke, personal communication 4/6/05).

This is all the more remarkable because of its similarity to conception dreaming in Aboriginal Australia, whereby *every* birth, not just those of religious specialists, is made possible via a spiritual encounter—usually by the father—in a dream (W. Shapiro 1979, 9–13).[1] My own research in northeast Arnhem Land revealed that here too multiple copulations are deemed necessary, the first to generate the fetus, others to maintain it during gestation; but only the woman's husband has sexual rights to her (W. Shapiro 1981, 16–20). This is often the case in Amazonia (see e.g. Basso 1973; Rivière 1969; Seeger 1981).[2] Moreover, the Aboriginal Australian notion whereby only one man generates the physical fetus and acts as an intermediary between the carnal and spiritual worlds has an Amazonian counterpart among the Trio of Suriname (Rivière 1974).

There are many variations on these themes. In the southwest of Arnhem Land the dual aspect of the paternal role is split, so that one man generates the physical fetus but another has the spiritual encounter (Stanner 1960, 254). Elsewhere (W. Shapiro 1988) I have argued that this division of labor is remarkably like the father/godfather complementarity in many Christian churches; and, in the same article, I noted that the more common Aboriginal Australian pattern, whereby genitor and dreamer are the same man, is echoed in Roman Catholic dogma up to the seventh century, positing as it did that the two roles—father and godfather—are played by the same man.

The necessity of repeated copulations has also been reported for the Trobriand Islands by Weiner (1988, 57–58), who notes that, by these acts, the father is supposed to provide form to the amorphous fetus generated, allegedly, by the mother and one of her matriclan spirits. Such imposition of form suggests *violence*, so it is not surprising to find paternity associated with violent action in other traditions—all the more so because of the substantial overlap between those portions of the brain activated during sex and those activated during aggression (Zillman 1984). Thus, Jay (1985, 1992), reviewing the literature on sacrifice in Subsaharan Africa and elsewhere, shows that coparticipation in ritual killing and eating ratifies the father/son bond as well as more extended kin ties derived from it. Much the same applies in Aboriginal Australia. Here, as noted, father and child are linked by the dream encounter, which in turn reflects connection to a mythic world in which existing order—in the dual sense of a formed landscape and a set of moral precepts—is established in the course of the self-sacrifice of Archetypical Beings (Munn 1970). There are South American counterparts. In Aztec sacrifice, the victim was said to be the "son" of his captor, who was therefore the former's "father" (Sahagún, quoted in Sanday 1986, 185). In Amazonia itself precisely the same metaphorical relationship pertains between the victim and his slayer in the cannibal raids of the Wari of southwestern Brazil (Conklin 2001a, 121, 2001b, 157; Vilaça 2002, 359). From this is seems but a short conceptual stretch to the "child"/"father" relationship linking a Roman Catholic layperson with his/her priest, who, by administering the Mass, reenacts an Archetypical Sacrificial Meal with each of his flock.

This is a by no means exhaustive enumeration. Still, it should suffice to show that partible paternity partakes of certain themes which have a very wide distribution in ethnographic space and historical time, including space and time that might be called "Western," and should therefore not, from a comparative standpoint, be essentialized. But this is not the only metaempirical strategy that Beckerman and Valentine employ. At the same time that they invoke its supposed "radical alterity," they claim also its *temporal priority* to what they construe as "Western" understandings. Thus, they speculate that "a good deal of human evolution may have been marked by a reproductive pattern in which semen from multiple mates may have been present at the same time in the female reproductive tract" (Beckerman and Valentine 2002b, 6–7). This is an astonishing claim. Even if the argument is open to question that the moderate degree of sexual dimorphism in *Homo sapiens* inclines us towards polygyny (Cachel n.d.), the fact remains that partible paternity has a distribution almost entirely limited to Amazonia and thus in no way satisfies the geographic requirements for great antiquity.[3] Yet Beckerman and Valentine are undeterred, speculating further that past "discussions of kinship theory . . . , while often discoursing on the application of the kin term for 'father' to many men, usually do not link this plural application of the label to an ideology of conception that allowed for a belief in biological plurality" (2002b, 9). This, if anything, is even more incredible; but since the study of systems of kin classification is no longer part of the anthropological canon, I need to provide a short and, I hope, relatively painless lesson on the topic.

In English we separate lineal ("direct line") from collateral ("on the side") kin by distinct terms. Thus, for female kin in the parental generation there is a woman we refer to as "mother" and other women—the mother's sister, say, and the father's sister—who we call "aunt." Similarly, for male kin in that generation, there is a man we refer to as "father," others—say the father's brother and the mother's brother—who are dubbed "uncle." English shares this pattern with most other Indo-European languages: in Castillian Spanish, for example, one's mother is *madre*, her sister and the father's sister *tia*; whereas one's father is *padre*, his brother and the mother's brother *tio*. The words differ but the pattern is identical. Just over sixty years ago Murdock

(1947), codifying knowledge that had already been secured for nearly a century, dubbed this parent-level sort of kin classification "lineal," because of its isolation of lineal from collateral kin, and its merging of the latter under a single term (or two terms, depending on gender).

I shall guess that, to most of us, lineal kin classification seems "natural," but in fact it is foreign to most of the world's languages. Thus, my own research in northeast Arnhem Land showed that an individual refers to his/her father as *bapa*, and that this term is also employed for the father's brother. The mother's brother, by contrast, is called *gawal* or *ngapipi*. As for parental generation females, the mother is *ngarndi* or *ngama*, as is her sister, but the father's sister is *mukul*. In short, from the standpoint of the individual doing the reckoning, parents' same-sex siblings are terminologically equated with the linking parent, while parents' opposite-sex siblings are not. Again codifying long-secured knowledge, Murdock (1947) called this pattern "bifurcate merging," because it *bifurcates* what for us is a single kin class ("uncle" or "aunt") and *merges* part of its membership with parental kin classes.

Note that *ngama* sound much like English "mama," and that *bapa* is phonologically nearly identical with English "papa." On the basis of a cross-cultural sample Murdock (1959) showed that such phonological similarities in unrelated languages occur much more commonly than one might expect by chance, given the range of the human vocal apparatus, when it comes to parental kin terms. Sounds like "mama," "papa," and "daddy" are of course among the easiest to make for a child just beginning to speak. Does this mean, then, that in populations with bifurcate merging kin classification the father's brother and the mother's sister are as significant in childcare as biological parents?[4]

To consider this question, I need to note that in such populations kin terms are applied to a wider circle of individuals than is the case in native English-speaking populations. Indeed, in many cases they are applied to everyone—what Barnard (1978) has called "universal systems of kin categorization". Aboriginal Australians are textbook examples of this tendency: in northeast Arnhem Land any woman one's mother calls "sister"—not just her actual sisters—can be called *ngama*, and any man one's father calls "brother"—not just his actual brothers—can be called *bapa*. Does this mean that in these populations everyone is regarded as kin? This is an especially important question here, because universal systems of kin categorization exist in Amazonia and, as I show below, Beckerman and Valentine have egregiously misrepresented them. The answer, as I have documented elsewhere (W. Shapiro 1979, 57–58, 1981, 41, 2005), is *very decidedly no*. Such populations are, in fact, much like our own in this regard, insofar as they posit notions remarkably similar to those we label "kin" (as opposed to "nonkin"), "relatives" (as opposed to "nonrelatives"), and "family" (as opposed to "outside the family").

I can now return to my childcare question. Since in populations with universal kin categorization there are so many "mothers" and "fathers," it would seem unlikely that all of them could be involved in caring for a child generated by only two of them, and in fact, *there is not a single instance in the ethnographic record of such a communal regime for the raising of children.* Such a regime was implicit in Morgan's fantasies about "group marriage," which he came to share, however unwittingly, with Engels. But, like other elements of Marxist societal planning, it has proved unworkable when attempted in practice, as in various communal "experiments" of the century recently passed (again see Brumann 2000; Shepher and Tiger 1975). And this is true because children bond with only a limited number of individuals (Flanagan 1999, 41 *et seq.*), and because the majority of fathers and most mothers wish to nurture their own offspring. Recent domestic trends aside, families do *not* come in all shapes and size, and it really does *not* take a village.

But could it take a body of more closely related individuals—what anthropologists call a "kindred?" As I have noted, such bodies exist in probably all populations with universal kin categorization; indeed, they most likely exist everywhere, as Scheffler (1973, 758) has suggested. And it is probably true everywhere that, especially when localized, as is usually the case in Amazonia (J. Shapiro 1984, 10–11), they have a greater salience in everyday life than do more widely dispersed collectivities that, under the logic of universal kin categorization, happen to get classed with kin. Thus, in northeast Arnhem Land, people in a residential group tend to be close kin (W. Shapiro 1973), and there is a certain amount of co-parenting. I can recall one young man who could not tell me which of his father's two wives was his biological mother: the two women were sisters, so he called both *ngama,* and because of their close association with each other, he had known both of them, in much the same capacity, for as long as he could remember. But although he could not answer it, my question was meaningful to him, for northeast Arnhem Landers have a variety of symbolic forms by which one's genetrix can be separated from all others of the *ngama* class, even her own sisters (for details, see W. Shapiro 1981, 87–89). Similarly, although men are close to their actual brothers—brothers are often married to sisters, and a younger brother is expected to take a man's wives upon his death—there are a number of ways by which an individual can distinguish his/her (presumed) genitor from the latter's brothers and all other occupants of the *bapa* class (W. Shapiro 2005, 51). For example, when asked simply to name his/her *bapa,* an individual nearly always nominates his/her (presumed) biological father, sometimes adding that this man is his/her 'true' (*yuwalk*) *bapa*. By implication, other members of the *bapa* class are less-than-true — which is to say that we are, once again, dealing with a matter of focality. Further, even when married brothers live together, which is far from always the case (W. Shapiro 1973, 376), each sleeps with his own wife or wives and their dependent children. I show below that all this — the conceptual and residential separation of one's parents from all others — is also true for Amazonia.

Let me now return to Beckerman and Valentine's remark whereby the plural application of the "father" term in bifurcate merging systems is linked to "a belief in biological plurality" — i.e. to partible paternity. This contention utterly ignores the issue of focality: it assumes, in other words, that all members of the "father" class in such systems are equally members of that class. Despite all the evidence for focality in other domains, and in lineal systems of kin classification ("Father Time," "Uncle Sam", my "mother country"), we are asked to believe that bifurcate merging schemes somehow do not partake of what appears to be a fundamental way by which the human brain organizes categories. But this is true neither in northeast Arnhem Land, as has been shown, nor in Amazonian populations with partible paternity, as I show below, nor anywhere else.[5]

Though empirical nonsense, the combination of "radical alterity" and historical priority claimed by Beckerman and Valentine for partible paternity has a familiar ring for students of the history of ideas, anthropological or otherwise. If, as Beckerman and Valentine allege, bifurcate merging kin classification is to be explained by partible paternity, what accounts for its existence in populations with no such ideology or practice? Beckerman and Valentine must surely know that partible paternity is by no means universal in Amazonia, and that it is almost all but unknown elsewhere. But if it is, as they speculate, an ideology and practice of great antiquity, greater, presumably, than "plain vanilla single paternity" (Beckerman and Valentine 2002b, 7), those populations with bifurcate merging kin classification that lack it must once have had it — as, indeed, we must all have. Lewis Henry Morgan has been resurrected — and on the very same problem! Just as Morgan, confronted with the widespread occurrence of bifurcate merging, resorted, also erroneously, to the mixed bag of phenomena that later anthropologists would call "unilineal descent groups," regarding them as historically prior to nuclear families, so Beckerman and Valentine evoke the specter of a once omnipresent partible paternity.[6] But Morgan considered Iroquois "clans" and Roman "gentes" to be retrograde in what he expressly called "moral evolution." It was not he, but Engels, who saw them as "early" stages of "evolution" to which the bourgeois "West" should — indeed, *must*, by "historical necessity" —

return. Beckerman and Valentine do not go quite so far, but it is to Engels' primitivism and not to Morgan's progressivism that they are indebted.

But this is not all. The Victorian Morgan was obsessed with sex, and he believed that "clans" and "gentes" signaled an earlier "stage" of "group marriage." Indeed, this fantasy was a staple of Victorian scholarship, which considered it morally repugnant, and it has been a recurrent fixation of social primitivists since at least Engels' day (Brumann 2000, 180–82; Stocking 1987, 316). Never mind that Thomas (1906), Malinowski (1913), and Lowie (1920, 61–62) demolished it ethnographically within the first two decades of the twentieth century: obsessions never really die. So it is perhaps unsurprising that two professional anthropologists, writing a century later and confronted with some data from a more recently Lost World, should resurrect "group marriage."

I hasten to add that this is not what Beckerman and Valentine expressly do: their focus instead is on the provisioning of mothers and their dependent children, which, they contend, is more effectively done by several men rather than by only one. But each of these several men may also, presumably, have several partners, all shared with several other men. This is nothing if not a twenty-first century "group marriage" fantasy.

Consider in this connection the adversarial relationships Beckerman and Valentine cultivate with Steven Pinker and E.O. Wilson. They quote Pinker (1997, 488–90):

> Sexual jealousy is found in all cultures . . . [I]n no society do men readily share a wife. A woman having sex with another man is *always* a threat to that man's genetic interests, because it might fool him into working for a competitor's genes (emphasis in original).

And here is part of their quote from Wilson (1998, 170): ". . . [I]n courtship men are predicted to stress exclusive sexual access and guarantees of paternity, while women consistently emphasize commitment of resources and material security." These arguments, they assert, "are called into question by decades of ethnographic research among tribal peoples in lowland south America" (Beckerman and Valentine 2002b, 4). The allegations, then, are that in Amazonia there is no male sexual jealousy, that men readily share their wives with other men, and that there is no concern with establishing some degree of paternal certainty. This is Morgan" worst nightmare, Engels' best fantasy, and, I show below, an utterly distorted reading of the Amazonian evidence.

Before proceeding to an examination of this evidence, I think it worthwhile to make several further points. First, it is necessary to show that men are *usually* concerned with the fidelity of their wives, not—as Wilson and especially Pinker seem to think—that they *always* are. A prediction like Wilson's, like other hypotheses derived from Darwinian theory—or for that matter, *any* scientific theory—may or may not be statistically validated, but, as noted above, there is no requirement that it hold true in every case. Which is to say that men sometimes *do* share their wives relatively willingly. One thinks immediately here of polyandry, which it should be noted, is exceedingly rare (Prince Peter 1963, 570) and which usually involves wife-sharing by brothers and other close kin successfully predicted by Darwinian theory to be unlikely to aggress against each other (Daly and Wilson 1988, 34–35). Melvin Goldstein, who worked in polyandrous communities in Tibet, found no instances of conflict among co-husbands (personal communication; see also LeVine 1988, 165). Similarly, Prince Peter (1963, 525) notes: "Very little jealousy is shown by any peoples living in polyandry." But his tabular summary of findings (1963, 527–47) indicates that sexual jealousy exists in all four of the clusters of communities he considered. A less equivocal set of examples from this standpoint are those populations in which spouse-exchange occurs, most famously among the Inuit, but also elsewhere, wherein men do indeed readily share wives, usually for purposes of economic alliance (see e.g. Burch 1975, 106–111; Guemple 1972, 59–62; Wallace 1969). Also pertinent here are "swingers' clubs" and related "alternate lifestyle" venues, in present-day North America and Western Europe, in which, it appears, sexual relations outside the pair-bond are tolerated only if they do not threaten that relationship (Jankowiak and Mixson 2008).

Second, since Beckerman and Valentine have plainly read Pinker and Wilson, their mix of "biophobia" and primitivism might be thought to be not so strong as it is with Lee, Gottlieb, and the "third sex" scholars. It is, nevertheless, very definitely present. Their "evolutionary" speculations on partible paternity are entirely without support and therefore constitute a primitivist fantasy, logically akin to Lee on "primitive communism." There is, moreover, the same *faux* awe at the supposed Higher Consciousness of "tribal" people that can be found in Lee's writings and those of the "third sex" researchers. Indeed, the alleged wisdom of such people is plainly presented as superior to that of Pinker and Wilson, who are, after all, evoked only to be bashed. A commitment to "plain-vanilla single paternity," which I shall guess that both Pinker and Wilson have, is extended from them to "the West" and considered sensually and imaginatively retrograde in comparison with partible paternity.

Here is my third point. One might say that, even if the Beckerman and Valentine analysis is deeply flawed, as I show below that it is, this has no great significance: an academic book published by a less-than-prestigious press is meant only for other academics, and its ideas are unlikely in the extreme to gain wider currency. But this has been anything but the fate of their essay. The volume in which it appears (Beckerman and Valentine 2002a) seems to have stemmed from an article published in *Current Anthropology* by Beckerman and several colleagues (Beckerman *et al* 1998), in which form it was apparently communicated to Meredith Small, a gifted popularizer of anthropological ideas. Small interviewed Beckerman and his associates for *Discover* magazine and from this generated a *Discover* article (Small 2003).[7] In her very first paragraph she says this:

> If biological fatherhood can be shared—an idea accepted by many indigenous groups across South America . . . —then the nuclear family with one mom and one dad might not be the established blueprint for a family that we have been led to expect. If so, the familiar story of traditional human mating behavior, in which the man the hunter brings home the bacon to his faithful wife, loses credibility. And if the [Amazonian] groups work perfectly well with more flexible family styles, the variety of family structures that are increasingly common in Western culture these days—everything from single-parent households to blended families—may not be as dangerous to the social fabric as we are led to believe. People in this culture may simply be exercising the same family options that humans have had for millions of years, options that have been operating in other cultures while the West took a stricter view of what constitutes a family (p. 86).

There is much more to this astonishing journalistic misrepresentation of ethnographic data, but the foregoing will suffice here. Note the fabrication of "the West" which we have already encountered, and the enhanced moral evaluation of the Rest, also encountered. Note too, the hostility to "Western" science, here charged with telling a "story" with conservative social implications. (Exactly why Small's article is not also a "story," though one with very different social implications, is not addressed.) And finally, there is the utterly gratuitous assimilation of occasional trysting—I show below that this is mostly what partible paternity in Amazonia is about—to radical alterations of domestic regime in the name of "flexibility." All this in a journal with about 700,000 subscribers![8]

But Small's is not the only path to popular appeal taken by Beckerman and his associates. Their ideas on partible paternity were initially presented at a 1999 symposium of the American Association for the Advancement of Science, at which the respected primatologist and evolutionary theorist Sarah Hrdy was present. Hrdy appears to have been much taken with their presentation, such that in her well-known book on maternal behavior partible paternity is briefly—though unspectacularly—discussed (Hrdy 1999, 246–49). Much the same can be said for her subsequent article in *Natural History*

(Hrdy 2001). But elsewhere she has been less subdued. A Leakey Foundation newsletter I discovered on the website leakeyfoundation.org/news & events quotes her as saying this of the Beckerman and Valentine volume: "This book challenges long-held dogma in fields like evolutionary psychology, anthropology, and sociobiology. People in these fields will now *have* to deal with partible paternity . . ." (emphases in original).

Other material I found via computer shows even less restraint. The same newsletter says that Beckerman and Valentine "have discovered a strong correlation between the status of women . . . and . . . multiple paternity." It quotes Valentine as saying the following: "The conventional view of the male-female bargain [in evolutionary studies] is that a man will provide food and shelter for a woman and her children if he can be assured that the children are biologically his. Our research turns this idea on its head, by showing that in reality there are many different modes of family life . . ." The website parents.org.uk rhetorically ask "When are two dads better than one?"—and provides the answer: "when the women are in charge, according to new research from [the] Amazonian rainforest." The Cambridge University website (cambridge.org.uk) plays only a little more loose with Beckerman and Valentine by stating that "the social acceptance of multiple fathers . . . contradicts previous notions of human universals that include sexual jealousy arising from concerns with paternal confidence." Finally, we learn from chaparraltree .com/honeyguide/subject-science-anthropology that partible paternity is at odds with evolutionary psychology: "One of the fundamental tenets of evolutionary psychology—the discipline that claims that certain cultural phenomena are universal because they have a hard-wired neurobiological basis— is the sanctity of female chastity . . . But it turns out that . . . female fidelity is not universal after all."

If must be an awfully naïve evolutionary psychologist who considers "the sanctity of female chastity" to be universal. As for the absence of sexual jealousy, I show below that Amazonian men are not quite so generous with their wives as some people—Beckerman and Valentine among them—seem to think; that these wives—or, more accurately, Amazonian women in general—are not nearly so respected as some of the Internet material suggests; and that Beckerman and Valentine's contention, noted above, that "there are many different modes of family life" is not at all supported by the Amazonian evidence. I would stress again that my concern is to show the applicability of focality theory and Darwinian theory to a particular problem, and with continuing the Enlightenment project of unmasking nonsense and misrepresentation. That Beckerman and Valentine are not, I presume, committed to every bit of flim-flam that has emerged from the reception of their book is besides the point, which is that, in any case, they have aided and abetted some of the most egregious distortions of the truth in the history of anthropology.

For the most part I consider the evidence by topic rather than by population. But, for reasons that will become clear shortly, I deal with the pertinent materials from the Northwest Amazon separately.

NOTES

1. Scheffler (1978, 7), reviewing the literature on various parts of Aboriginal Australia, points out that fetal quickening or birth is the occasion of the dream experience, though much of the theoretical literature has it as conception. It is not necessary to argue the matter here.

2. Seeger (1981, 123) has this to say: "The Suya believe that a child is created through the repeated intercourse of the same man with a particular woman. Emphasis is placed on the repetition—it takes a lot of semen to build a child—and on the unitary nature of the genitor." But in a personal communication to me dated 5/30/05 he notes as follows: "Many Suya do seem to subscribe to a kind of partible paternity but also say that one man usually contributes more than the others." Writing of the Ese Eja, Lepri (2005, 722) notes that "young mothers were adamant that one copulation was sufficient to make a baby." What is involved here, clearly, is the sort of "intracultural variation" that pertains especially to conception ideologies, as already noted. The idea that some populations "have" partible paternity and others do not may well be misleading: even among those who "have" it, its behavioral importance varies. I take this up again below.

3. Appeal here is made to the "age-area" principle, which holds that more widely distributed traits are older than those of lesser distribution. It seems still to survive in some fields, though at least in this country the emergence of the subdiscipline of "cultural anthropology" from "ethnology" signaled its disappearance. Its application of greatest importance for present purposes is Lowie (1920, 147–57) on the antiquity of the nuclear family.

4. I use the word "population" because it suggests groups of people, the subject of this book. "Culture" and "society," by contrast, present operational problems which need not be dealt with here.

5. Precisely the same error was made by so-called "alliance theorists" in the 1950s, 1960s, and early 1970s, who maintained or assumed that "father" terms in what they called "prescriptive marriage systems" had in fact nothing to do with paternity. (For a seminal critique see Scheffler and Lounsbury 1971, 14–35). Their deeply flawed analyses have more recently been resurrected with utter fidelity by Parkin (1997) in an introductory text. This signals a decided didactic irresponsibility on his part, and a complete inability to learn from his peers (W. Shapiro 1995). Worse yet, he has combined with Linda Stone in another venture (Parkin and Stone 2004); Stone's own feminist-oriented text (first edition 1997) pays virtually no attention to the focality issue in any of its (at the moment) three editions. We thus have, masqueraded as the best of

secured knowledge and the best of new venues in tandem, one of the discipline's most egregious scholarly and pedagogical failures of recent years.

6. In fact, Morgan's own data (Morgan 1871), as Lounsbury (1969, 133–34) pointed out nearly a century later, showed that, when considered in more detail, bifurcate merging systems are not at all isomorphic with unilineal descent groups. There is some irony here in that around the same time as Lounsbury put forward his argument, ethnographies began to appear, from Amazonia and elsewhere, emphasizing the occurrence of bifurcate merging in populations without unilineal descent groups (e.g. Overing Kaplan 1975; Rivière 1969; Yalman 1967). It remains to be explained why the two are associated to a degree beyond chance (Murdock 1947).

7. I read Small's article in reprinted form in *Annual Editions: Anthropology 05/06*, edited by Elvio Angelini and published by McGraw-Hill/Dushkin. Pagination refers to this forum

8. According to telephone information form *Discover*'s editorial office obtained 1/17/06. It is worth noting here that the line between scholarly and popular anthropology, if it ever existed, is thinner now than ever before. It seems to be rhetorically drawn to discredit scholars whose views are taken to be right-of-center, as when E.O. Wilson's credentials as an entomologist are invoked, with the implication that he is not professionally qualified to say anything about human beings. Note too, Small's use of the buzz-words "Man the hunter." Though initially employed by the Marxist Richard Lee (Lee and DeVore 1968), they have become a *bête noir* of feminists because of their supposed androcentric connotations.

Chapter Three

The Northwest Amazon Cases

Some of the most revealing data of present relevance from this area comes from Valentine's own research among the Curripaco of Colombia (Valentine 2002). The native lexicon distinguishes between what Valentine (2002, 185) translates as the "major father" of a child and his/her "lesser fathers." Note immediately that this distinction is one of focality: the "major father" is *ipso facto* more "fatherish" than "lesser fathers." The former is "the man with whom the mother has had the most sex, and who therefore contributes the most seminal fluid to the formation of the fetus" (*ibid.*). For the former reason he is—though Valentine fails to note this—most likely to be the biological father. In other words, the degree of paternal uncertainty here is considerably diminished— just as evolutionary psychology would predict. Further evidence in the same direction is provided by the fact that premarital pregnancy is regarded as an embarrassment for which a girl's father (presumably, her mother's husband) and brothers may beat her (Valentine 2002, 186), that her marriage is arranged (*ibid.*, 182), and that extramarital sex is ideally limited to men of her husband's patrikin group (*ibid.* 189). Even so, the "major father"/"lesser father" distinction remains, with the former position, apparently, usually if not always filled by the husband himself.[1] And when brothers do share sexual access to the same woman, they do not always do so harmoniously. Valentine's words:

> . . . [T]hese relationships can be unstable. Brothers do compete for wives, and if one is successful, the others may resent him. In one instance, which is unraveling at the moment, one brother is turning against his sibling in fits of jealousy, throwing scorn on him for . . . not finding a woman of his own. He says he would kill him if he were [less closely related] . . . If these drunken brawls continue everyone agrees [that] the village will divide and the brothers separate (2002, 189).

Such reluctance to aggress against a brother, and the far greater readiness to do so against someone less closely related, is also consistent with findings in evolutionary psychology (Daly and Wilson 1988, 34–35).

Moreover, the "major father" is expected to undergo certain restrictions, especially fasting, at the birth of his child and for the child's supposed benefit. This cluster of restrictions, especially common in Amazonia, has become part of the anthropological canon as "the couvade." In this connection, Valentine (2002, 188) also notes the following:

> Lesser fathers do not have to fast. As "they do not think of the baby," nor want it, nor feel responsible for it, they can do it no harm. By not fasting they relinquish all claims to [being] the major father. They have no place in the marriage.

As the major father, the mother's husband is joined in the couvade by his wife (Valentine 2002, 187)—which is to say that the collectivity of man, woman, and dependent child is symbolically isolated.[2] Another part of this symbolic isolation is a "special diet," and an avoidance of subsistence activities, on the part of the mother and the major father. Hence to sustain themselves they need the assistance of kin. But, Valentine (2002, 188) notes, "[k]in of secondary fathers have no place here." It would be helpful to have more detail on Valentine's assertion that lesser fathers "do not think of the baby, nor want it, nor feel responsible for it," as well as on the spatial isolation of the bonded couple (Valentine 2002, 180), but it seems nonetheless plain that what we have here is very far indeed from "group marriage," and, absent the couvade, surprisingly close to understandings that might be dubbed "Western."

Also highly pertinent are Janet Chernela's findings for the Wanano of the Brazilian Northwest Amazon (Chernela 1984, 1993, 2002, personal communication). Here, although the general bifurcate merging plan of kin classification holds, one's father's brothers are called by the "father" term supplemented by certain suffixes—these dependent upon age relative to the father (Chernela 1993, 63, 2002, 165). Which is to say that the father is the focal member of his kin class. This is especially significant because a man's brothers are the most likely secondary sexual partners of his wife (Chernela 1984, 31, 2002, 168, personal communication), yet their status in the "father" kin class is nonetheless derived: this is reminiscent of the Curripaco distinction between the "major father" and "lesser fathers." Moreover, as with the Curripaco, even among brothers there is sexual jealousy. Chernela's words:

> The casual extramarital encounters married women carry out are normally conducted with extreme discretion. "Raw" sex, sex with a partner other one's own spouse, should be kept at a distance from the parameters of the domestic space,

within which the monogamous unit is an integral element in the configuration of daily social life (Chernela 2002, 169; see also Chernela 1984, 31).

Note again the isolation of the bonded pair. The metaphorical rendition of extramarital sex as "raw" presumably implies illicitness, of uncivilized nature. Here Chernela notes that such trysting takes place in "remote gardens" (2002, 169). Most of these, she continues

> . . . contain makeshift overhangs or lean-tos to which hammocks can be attached, making conventional trysting places. The spatial demarcation between field and homesite differentiates the official from the unofficial, the legitimate from the casual, the social from the nonsocial. No indication of an affair should be registered publicly (*ibid.*)

And, in the same vein:

> Relations with illicit lovers are expected to be fleeting. An [extramarital] attraction that persists over time is regarded as dangerous and lovers who are visibly infatuated with [each other] are ridiculed. Any indication of preoccupation with a sexual partner, such as . . . frequency of meeting, is likely to be interpreted as an indication of sorcery (Chernela 2002, 170).

A woman's sexual life is thus focused on her husband, though not to the exclusion of his brothers. Which is to say that, again, paternal uncertainty is reduced. And if extramarital affairs between a man's wife and his brothers are tolerated if they are carried out surreptitiously, trysts with men less closely related can result in "bitter enmity" (Chernela 2002, 174; see also Chernela 1993, 130).

Also pertinent from the perspective of Marxist theory is the Wanano's low evaluation of women, whose marriages they arrange (Chernela 1993, 55–58) and whose sexuality they devalue. In one of her personal communications to me Chernela notes that

> . . . women are considered to be the more voracious [sexually] and they are blamed for all indiscretions . . . A woman can complain about her bachelor son if he is carrying on too much with married women. It is the men who are expected to have more self-control.

And: "[S]ex is considered debilitating to men and therefore they should not give in to the appetites of women too often" (and see Chernela 1984, 28). In one of her publications she goes into more detail on this last matter:

> [W]anano men view women as divisive and chaotic influences, especially through their uncontrolled, critical gossip. The [W]anano place extreme value

on style of speech, and men distinguish between the eloquent, decorous speech of men and the undisciplined unthinking chatter of women. Lack of restraint, in the male view, extends to female sexuality: woman is the seductress, the seeker of sex . . . Woman's anatomy is threatening. The ravenous female of an important myth devours a man's penis in her vagina. . . . Woman's body endangers and defiles the intellectual rigor and spiritual discipline practiced by [W]anano men (Chernela 1984, 29).

Moreover, menstruating woman are considered dangerous, at least to shamans (Chernela 1993, 131). If effective, such ideologies of sexual pollution would further decrease paternal uncertainty. But even if they are not, it is clear that the emancipation of women imagined by Engels has yet to reach the Northwest Amazon. This conclusions is captured in a nutshell by the data that Wanano villages are ranked, and women of high-ranking villages are said to be "like men" (Chernela, 1993, 140; see also Chernela 1985). Finally, in one of her personal communications to me, Chernela mentions "a flute ritual to which women are forbidden" (personal communication 12/29/05). I show below that similar ritual complexes elsewhere in Amazonia betoken a remarkable denigration of women.

Now the Curripaco, the Wanano, and other native populations of the Northwest Amazon have something like "patrilineal descent groups." These are not, to be sure, the classic "segmentary lineage" systems made famous by ethnographers working in Africa in the 1930s, 1940s, and later, whose findings were summarized in a classic article by Fortes (1953). Rather, although individual membership is derived from one's father, the ideology of these groups is otherwise non-genealogical. There is little if any of the "tracing of descent" mentioned in textbook introductions to kinship studies. Instead, there is a posited this world/other world dichotomy, with the latter half seen as temporally prior to, and mystically generative of, the former—what Murphy (1979, 224), writing of Amazonia more generally, has called "a kind of descent that incorporates within itself qualities of timelessness." This is also true of the so-called "descent groups" of Aboriginal Australia (W. Shapiro 1979, 13–20) and of Native North America (Tooker 1971).[3] But this did not stop Morgan—and many others after him—from taking Iroquois "clans" as exemplars of "matrilineal kinship," or from founding a progressivist ladder whose rungs were "matriliny," "patriliny," and "cognatic kinship."

Another problem with this pseudo-historical typology is that it presumes that the bilateral reckoning of kinship is absent with "matriliny" and "patriliny" (however construed), whereas we now know, quite to the contrary, that it is very nearly universal: among the "matrilineal" Iroquois there are important ties with the father and his people, just as, among the "patrilineal" Northwest Amazonians, ties to the mother and her people are posited and are significant for certain purposes (Keesing 1975, 22).

In spite of these advances in our knowledge of human kinship, Beckerman and Valentine seem to cling to Morgan's—and Engels'—simplistic trichotomy. I need to quote the former pair at some length:

> In small egalitarian horticultural societies . . . , women's reproductive interests are best served if mate choice is a non-binding female decision; if there is a network of multiple females to aid or substitute for a woman in her mothering responsibilities; if male support for a woman and her children comes from multiple men; and if a woman is shielded from the effects of male sexual jealousy. Male reproductive interests, contrariwise, are best served by male control over female sexual behavior, promoting paternal certainty . . . This [latter] profile implies that . . . marriage is a lifetime commitment and extramarital affairs by women are severely sanctioned; and that this state of affairs is maintained by disallowing women reliable female support networks, or male support other than that of the husband . . .
> . . . [N]either sex can ever fully win this contest, yet there are situations that give the advantage to one or the other. Where women clearly hold the upper hand, . . . they choose their own husbands . . . ; women have broad sexual freedom both before and after marriage; the idea of partible paternity is prominent, with women having wide latitude in choosing the secondary father of their children; women usually make no secret of these secondary fathers . . . ; and the ideology of partible paternity defuses . . . potential conflicts between male rivals (Beckerman and Valentine 2002b, 11).

And, they add, several populations to be considered below "fit this description to a greater or lesser extent" (*ibid.*). On the other hand,

> Where men clearly dominate, patrilineality [is] the order of the day; women's husbands are typically chosen by their male relatives; partible paternity, if it is admitted at all as a biological possibility, tends to be rare . . . ; women often conceal the identity of secondary fathers of their children; and male sexual jealousy constitutes an ongoing potential danger to women (Beckerman and Valentine 2002b, 11–12.

Beckerman and Valentine add that [t]he Curripaco . . . and the Wanano are reasonably close to this pole . . ." (*ibid.*).

There are innuendos here that badly need elucidation. Thus, what is meant by the expression "secondary fathers?" If more than one man is held to sire a child, in what sense is one father primary, the other(s) "secondary?" Beckerman and Valentine say nothing about this, but I suspect strongly that they have in mind the sort of distinction made by the Curripaco between the "the major father" and "lesser fathers," and which, as we shall see, is extremely common in Amazonia. But, if so, one might expect some treatment of the focality issue, which Beckerman and Valentine do not provide. By not doing so, they give the impression that paternal privileges and responsibilities are equally distributed among supposed genitors, and this is simply not so: we have already seen this in the Northwest Amazon cases, and, as I show below, it holds for virtually all the others.

Also obscure is the argument for causation. Beckerman and Valentine's wording makes it seem as if gender hierarchy *simpliciter* is the causal factor responsible for their two clusters of traits: "Where woman have the upper hand . . ." They may not intend this, but such idiomization, coupled with an ignorance of the focality issue, feeds all too readily into the current state of siege in "Western" gender warfare.

Lest this be thought a rash conclusion, let me tabulate the alleged clusters. Before so doing I need to add something. Their second cluster includes "uxorilocal residence" (Beckerman and Valentine 2002b, 11)—which is to say that, upon marriage, the couple resides with the wife's parents and/or siblings. Systemically practiced, this leads to residential assemblages whose stable core consists of matrilineally related females. Whether or not matrilineal descent categories exist in Amazonia is a matter of some controversy (see esp. W. Crocker 1979), but this, I suspect, is of no consequence to those who would read into Beckerman and Valentine's presentation conclusions that in fact have nothing to do with Native South America. Herewith my tabulation in Table 3.1.

Engels would have loved this Manichean scheme, as would today's "radical" feminists. In the following chapters I show that, when applied to Amazonian ethnography, it is utter nonsense.

Table 3.1.   My Tabulation

men dominant	women dominant
stable marriage	unstable marriage
women's sexual partners chosen by others	women choose own sexual partners
partible paternity absent or limited	flourishing partible paternity
"sisterhood" powerless (patrilineality)	"sisterhood" powerful (matrilineality)
pair bond clearly defined	pair bond submerged by other ties
male sexual jealousy rampant	male sexual jealousy checked

NOTES

1. I take this very decidedly non-Marxist concern with controlling women's sexuality to be general in Amazonia, because Amazonian ethnographers do. In most of the literature the mother's husband is routinely referred to as "the father" of her children—even when issues of partible paternity are discussed and nearly always otherwise. I provide below further evidence for the importance of the conjugal tie throughout the area.

2. I avoid throughout this analyses the expression "nuclear family," except when quoting others. It will subsequently become clear that this unit is in fact residentially and symbolically isolated throughout Amazonia, but there is no need to beg the question of its "nuclear" quality here.

3. In the Judaeo-Christian tradition much the same this world/other world generative relationship exists, though with "segmentary lineage" notions: witness Biblical genealogies, at the end of which is posited an ontological gap between "then" and "now." This "segmentary" quality almost certainly is related to the geographical situation of the Ancient Hebrews and their pastoral economy: present-day Arabs and other Muslim peoples of the Middle East manifest this quality in earnest.

Chapter Four

Other Pertinent Cases: General Considerations[1]

As noted above, I shall consider the remainder of the evidence topic-by-topic. A detailed—though by no means exhaustive—examination of the pertinent Amazonian literature suggests the following topical breakdown: (1) evidence pertaining to focality in kin classification *simpliciter*; (2) evidence pertaining to focality in kin classification in connection with partible paternity; (3) evidence pertaining to the residential and symbolic isolation of the sexually bonded pair and dependent offspring; (4) evidence pertaining to sexual jealousy; (5) evidence pertaining to the denigration and subordination of women; and (6) miscellaneous evidence. It should, perhaps, be recalled here that the Marxist Paradise to which Beckerman and Valentine lend themselves all too readily supposes that the sexually bonded pair and dependent offspring are submerged in communitarian bliss wherein all members of a kin class are equally members of that class (hence the relevance of topics 1–3); that sexual jealousy does not exist (topic 4); and that there is gender equality (topic 5). By contrast, I show below that Amazonian communities are very decidedly divided—and this along lines not at all unfamiliar to those of us used to "Western" understandings; that sexual jealousy is rampant in Amazonia; and that, in this region, women are remarkably denigrated in a wide variety of behavioral and ideological ways. Which is to say that the Northwest Amazon situation is by no means unique. To these ends I have tabulated (Table 4.1) the populations to be considered, using the ethnographic labels most frequently encountered in the literature.[2]

Table 4.1.   Names and Locations of Amazonian Populations with Partible Paternity Outside the Northwest Amazon (for references, see text)

Ache	Eastern Paraguay
Apinayé	Central Brazilian savanna
Araweté	Central Brazilian rainforest
Barí	Colombian Amazon and adjoining parts of Venezuela
Bororo	Central Brazilian savanna
Canela	Eastern Brazilian savanna
Cashinahua	Peruvian Amazon and adjoining parts of Brazil
Ese Eja	Bolivian Amazon and adjoining parts of Peru
Guajá	Eastern Brazilian rainforests
Huaorani	Ecuadorian Amazon
Kawahiv	Western Brazilian rainforest
Kayapó	Central Brazilian savanna
Krahó	Central Brazilian savanna
Kuikuru	Central Brazilian rainforest
Kulina	Peruvian Amazon and adjoining parts of Brazil
Matis	Western Brazilian rainforest
Mehinaku	Central Brazilian rainforest
Sharanahua	Peruvian Amazon
Tapirapé	Central Brazilian savanna
Warao	Orinoco delta region
Wari	Western Brazilian rainforest
Yanomami	Brazil/Venezuela border
Yukpa	Colombia/Venezuela border
Yuquí	Bolivian Amazon

NOTES

1. In none of the cases considered here is there good evidence for localized patrilineal groups. Chagnon's attempts to claim them for the Yanomami have been criticized by Murphy (1979, 219–21) and others.

2. I have omitted the Siriono of the Bolivian Amazon (Holmberg 1969) and the Waiwai of the Brazil/Guyana border region (Fock 1963) because it is not entirely clear that these populations have an ideology of partible paternity (but see Chapter 2 Note 2).

Chapter Five

Evidence Re Focality in Kin Classification *Simpliciter*

In bifurcate merging systems outside Amazonia primary kin—one's parents, siblings, and children—are usually if not always singled out as the focal members of their kin classes, probably most commonly by adjectival forms translatable as "true" or "real" (W. Shapiro 2005, 50–53). This is one way in which the sexually bonded pair and its offspring are separated from the rest of the community. In point of fact, this is precisely the case for those Amazonian systems of kin classification for which adequate information is available, and I am aware of not a single exception. The best published data come from Kensinger's elegant analyses of subclassification in Cashinahua kinship and other domains (Kensinger 1984a, 1995, 83 *et seq.*), but there is corroboration for the Apinayé (Da Matta 1973, 280), the Guajá (Cormier 2003, 79), the Kayapó (Fisher 2003, 121), the Wari (Aparecida Vilaça. personal communication), and the Yanomami (Chagnon 1988, 35; Peters 1998, 114; Ramos and Albert 1976, 82). It seems also to exist among the Tapirapé: Judith Shapiro (1968, 10) reports that an intensifying suffix can be added to at least some kin terms to distinguish close kin from others.[1]

A related pattern is the addition of a (usually) diminutive suffix to a kin term to signal nonfocal application. This is so common ethnographically that, over a half century ago, Murdock (1957, 673) gave it a special typological label, "derivative bifurcate merging." Thus, a father's brother, though a "father" in a looser sense, can be rendered as "a little father"—or, more accurately, "a little bit father."[2] In Amazonia this pattern has been reported for the Araweté (Viveiros de Castro 1992, 15), the Kawahiv (Kracke 1978, 15, 1984, 101), the Krahó (Melatti 1979, 53), the Kulina (Pollock 2002, 54–55), the Tapirapé (J. Shapiro 1968, 3; Wagley 1977, 97), the Warao (Heinen 1972, 43; Suarez 1971, 84), and the Wari (Conklin 2001a, 118–19). For the Guajá, a woman other than the genetrix who nurses a child is referred to as a the child's "other mother," i.e. her classification is logically dependent upon or *derived from* that of the genetrix.

There are still other ways by which parents and/or other close kin are separated from those less closely related in these populations. Among the Tapirapé there is a special term "used by young children . . . to address the father; this term is never used for the paternal uncle" (J. Shapiro 1968, 8). Presumably this expression indicates special emotional closeness, though this is not expressly stated. By contrast, a correspondingly isolating term among the Apinayé is said to connote "intimacy and affection" (Da Matta 1979, 92).

In universal system of kin categorization parents probably always provide the focal points for the wider application of kin terms. Thus, in northeast Arnhem Land I found that someone applies a kin term to another usually based on what his/her father and/or mother calls that other, or that other's father or mother (W. Shapiro 1981, 36–37). Among the populations considered here, much the same logic is expressly reported for the Araweté (Viveiros de Castro 1992, 156–58) and the Warao (Heinen 1972, 44) and is implied in all other cases. Note, by contrast, that the application of kin terms to parents and children derives from the procreative relationship *simpliciter* and is thus independent of other kin links. These relationships are thus the true "elementary structures of kinship" (Scheffler 1973, 749–51).

In such universal systems, moreover, expressions are also common which collectively separate kin from others, often with an indication that these others, though occupants of kin classes, are not really kin at all (W. Shapiro 2005). Such expressions have been reported for Amazonia for the Apinayé (Da Matta 1979, 87–90), the Cashinahua (Kensinger 1995, 153; McCallum 2001, 28), the Kayapó (Bamberger 1979, 135), the Krahó (Melatti 1979, 61), the Kulina (Pollock 2002, 44), the Mehinaku (Gregor 1977, 261–63), the Sharanahua (Siskind 1973, 50), the Warao (Suarez 1971, 90), and the Wari (Conklin 2002, 215; Vilaça 2000, 94–95). The Cashinahua, in addition, have expressions which separate primary kin from collateral kin (Kensinger 2002, 16). For the Warao, Heinen (1972, 43) reports that half-siblings can be rendered as having "one father, different mother . . . or vice versa," in contrast to full siblings who have "one father, one mother." These expressions employ the native parent terms in their linguistically unmarked or unmodified sense, suggesting that parents are indeed the focal members of the classes designated by these terms.[3] Heinen (*ibid.*) further notes—and this is unusual for Amazonia—that "there is not a gradual transition but a definite hiatus between kinsmen and those who are not." Finally, there is a succinct statement by Viveiros de Castro (1991, 160) that "the Araweté do *not* consider all members of the group 'relatives' to whom kinship terms are applied" (emphases in original).

Lepri (2005, 721) reports that among the Ese Eja, "the terms for classificatory kin are sometimes qualified with [a] suffix . . . meaning 'like,' as in 'like a brother.'" She notes further that, although kin-like links can be forged through sex and living and eating together, the consubstantiality that derives from these acts "remains open to denial" (2005, 710). There are parallels on both counts among the Wari (Conklin 2001a, 118, 121).

NOTES

1. Compare English "this very day" (as opposed to "sooner or later").

2. I prefer my rendition because it indicates the nonfocal nature of the subclass. There are systems of kin classification wherein a father's *younger* brother is a "little father," but this is another matter.

3. In systems of kin classification generally, the use of a kin term in its unmarked sense indicates focality. Thus, in English when I speak of "my father" it is obvious that I am *not* referring to a Roman Catholic priest or to Father Time. For a general statement of marking theory in semantics, see Kronenfeld (1996, 89–113).

Chapter Six

Evidence Re Focality in Kin Classification Stemming from Partible Paternity

The foregoing chapter takes no account whatsoever of subclassification in kinship owing to partible paternity. Indeed, it might be thought that, with this ideology, "father" and other kin terms are applied with the same significance to all those deemed to be connected to an individual via the same ethnoembryological route. But this is not at all the case. We have already seen that the Curripaco distinguish between "the major father" and "lesser fathers," assigning to the former—and focal—subclass the man who has the most sex with the mother. Precisely this distinction is also made by the Yanomami. Here is Àles (2002, 70) on the matter:

> . . . [A] kind of hierarchy is established [among] the different co-progenitors. The husband is always assumed to have participated to the greatest extent in the conception of the fetus, and the [mother's lovers] have only "helped." Thus, the husband is . . . credited with the predominant part of the engendering of the child.

The Yanomami idiomize this distinction in terms of the "elder father"/ "younger father" contrast. Here it needs to be noted that in systems of kin classification generally "elder" status signals focality, "younger" nonfocality (Scheffler and Lounsbury 1971, 75). This generalization is supported by the Yanomami data. Here is Àles (2002, 70–71) in more detail:

> Co-paternity is accounted for in three distinct ways, each with its own logic. "Elder" and "younger" paternity can be attributed in such a way that the elder father . . . is the husband, with the younger father being the "nonhusband" co-father . . . ; the elder father . . . is the co-father who has participated quantitatively to a greater degree in the fabrication of the embryo, with the younger father . . . being he who has contributed less; the elder father . . . was the first to

have had sexual intercourse with the mother, and hence was the first to begin the fabrication of the embryo, while the younger father . . . had sexual intercourse with the mother . . . after the . . . creation of the fetal substance had already been initiated. This is irrespective of the number of instances of sexual intercourse: even if he had intercourse with the mother on numerous occasions after the first progenitor, the second partner is still the younger father and it is considered that he only "assisted" in the creation of the fetus.

All three criteria imply a sort of "primacy," i.e. focality, in contrast to a sort of secondary or nonfocal status. And what is involved here is a primacy of sexual access, which, as we saw in the Curripaco case, marks off the most likely genitor.

The Ache employ the second of these three criteria to make a similar distinction. Hill and Hurtado (1996, 274) report that "[t]he man who had most frequent sexual intercourse in the month prior to a woman's first missed period . . . is named as the 'real father' or 'the one who put the child in,'" and they note Ache expressions for this position which they translate as "primary father." And they add: "He is probably in most cases the genetic father of the child in question" (*ibid.*). Finally, they observe that "most primary fathers are men who are involved in a long-term recognized marriage and mating relationship with the mother of a child, whereas secondary fathers tend to be men who have temporary and/or hidden relations (premarital or extramarital) with the mother of the child" (Hill and Hurtado 1996, 274–275). Which is, of course, a statistical statement of the first criterion for primary fatherhood noted by Àles for the Yanomami.

It is this first criterion that figures most commonly in Amazonia in the partitioning of the "father" class into focal and nonfocal members with regard to partible paternity. The idea that the mother's husband is the primary (major, etc.) father has been reported for the Barí (Beckerman *et al* 2002, 32), the Kulina (Pollock 2002, 55–56), the Tapirapé(J. Shapiro 1968, 7), the Warao (Heinen 1972, 33; Heinen and Wilbert 2002, 215), and the Wari (Conklin 2001a, 119), and strongly suggested for the Bororo (J. Crocker 1979, 59), the Ese Eja (Peluso and Boster 2002, 145), and the Matis (Erikson 2002, 128). William Fisher and Terence Turner (personal communications) tell me that this is usually the case among the Kayapó. Finally, Turner (personal communication) informs me that, in genealogical elicitations, Kayapó informants readily nominated the mother's husband as the primary father, something also noted by Laura Rival (personal communication) for the Huaorani. This ease of nomination is a datum of the sort that figures regularly in research on focality (D'Andrade 1995, 109, 188).

The Mehinaku employ a variant of the second criterion noted above for the Yanomami. Unlike the cases just noted, they do not dichotomize the "father" class when it comes to partible paternity (Thomas Gregor, personal communication). Instead, they appear to treat it as having a continuous membership: a man who has sex with a woman only occasionally is said to be a "little bit" father to her children (Gregor, 1977, 293).

The Yuquí, on the other hand, all but exclude men other than the mother's husband from consideration. In a personal communication to me dated 1/17/06 Allyn Stearman has this to say: "The belief is that the husband actually conceives the child (even though the wife may spend time with other men), while the others just help it grow with their semen. These other men are not given any special name/title or even attention."

The only case I am aware of in which there is no lexical distinction here is the Canela. Although W.H. Crocker (1984, 71, 1990, 257; Crocker and Crocker 1994, 83) distinguishes between "fathers" and "contributing fathers" (or "co-fathers"), he notes expressly that the latter, like the former, are said to be "primary" rather than "secondary" members of the "father" kin class. Yet he also observes that the role of the mother's husband "is far more outstanding and distinct in its responsibilities . . ." (*ibid.*). More specifically, couvade restrictions for the mother's husband "are more extensive" than those maintained by "contributing fathers" (W. Crocker 2002, 88). The former is thus said to have "the principal role in strengthening the baby" (*ibid.*; see also W. Crocker 1984, 90; Nimuendajú 1946, 107).

W.H. Crocker (1990, 248) does note a Canela lexical distinction between "spouse" and "other spouse," the latter pertaining to a man's or woman's paramour—and, it needs to be stressed, a *nonfocal* member of the "spouse" category (see also Crocker and Crocker (1994, 71)). A comparable distinction has also been reported for the Ache (Clastres 1974, 319) and, less clearly, for the Yanomami (Peters 1998, 116).

Chapter Seven

Evidence Re the Residential and Symbolic Isolation of the Sexually Bonded Pair and Dependent Offspring

The most common pattern of such residential isolation involves the spatial separation of this unit within a more inclusive edifice or local community. This is reported for the Ache (Hill and Hurtado 1996, 65), the Apinayé (Da Matta 1979, 97, 1982, 41 *et seq.*), the Bororo (J. Crocker 1979, 291), the Canela (W. Crocker 1990, 238; 2002, 98; Nimuendajú 1946, 41), the Cashinahua (McCallum 2001, 60), the Guajá (Cormier 2003, 76), the Huaorani (Rival 1998, 621), the Kawahiv (Kracke 1978, 28, 1984, 113), the Kayapó (Fisher 2002, 126; Lea 1995, 207; Turner 1979, 180), the Kuikuru (Dole 1984, 46), the Mehinaku (Gregor 1977, 269), the Tapirapé (Wagley 1977, 87), the Warao (Heinen 1972, 25; Suarez 1971, 58–59), the Wari (Conklin 2001a, 17), the Yanomami (Peters 1998, 118), the Yukpa (Halbmayer 2004, 148), and the Yuquí (Stearman 1989, 94). *There is not a single report of a woman's or a man's paramours co-resident with her or him.*

In some of these instances, the conjugal pair constitutes a separate subsistence unit. This is reported for the Apinayé (Da Matta 1979, 97), the Bororo (J. Crocker 1985, 79), the Cashinahua (McCallum 2001, 60), the Guajá (Cormier 2003, 69), the Huaorani (Rival 2002, 105), the Kayapó (Lea 2002, 114), the Kuikuru (Carneiro 1958, 135; Dole 1969, 108), and the Warao (Suarez 1971, 60). In the same vein, Gregor (1977, 282), writing of the Mehinaku, observes: "Husband and wife . . . must bathe together at least once a day, share utensils, use appropriate kin-terms, sleep in adjacent hammocks, and participate in other stereotyped scenes that present their relationship to the rest of the community" (see also Gregor 1974).

Another symbolization is that the bonded pair and their children are consubstantial to a greater extent than with others. This is noted for the Apinayé

(Da Matta 1973, 279–80, 1979, 89), the Bororo (J. Crocker 1985, 81), and the Kayapó (Fisher 1998, 54–55, 2003, 123). Among the Canela (W. Crocker 1979, 237, 1984, 82), and the Wari (Conklin 2001a, 117–18), by contrast, consubstantiality extends to the mother's paramours. Yet even in these latter two cases the woman's husband seems to be more substantially connected than her lovers to her and her children. I have already shown this for the Canela. As for the Wari, Conklin (2001a, 117) notes that they hold that "the most direct bodily connections are those reinforced on a daily basis among parents and children who sleep and eat together."

It is this consubstantiality that, probably everywhere in Amazonia, underlies the couvade. I have already noted that, for the Canela, those chiefly restricted in this manner are the woman and her husband. This seems also to hold for the Apinayé (Da Matta 1979, 103–04, 1982, 53–57), the Kawahiv (Kracke 1981, 108), the Kayapó (Terence Turner, personal communication), the Krahó (Melatti 1979, 58), and the Wari (Conklin 2001a, 117–18). In this last case, Conklin (2001a, 118) states that the woman's paramours are supposed to observe these restrictions. But she quickly adds as follows: "Shamans sometimes use this idea as an indirect way to censure adultery, for when an adulterous woman's child gets sick, a shaman often will blame her child's illness on an animal killed by her lover" (*ibid.*). This, presumably, stems from the following consideration: "When a hunter has sex with a nursing mother, harmful spirit elements contained in his semen may enter her blood, pass into her breast milk, and contaminate her baby's blood" (*ibid.*). Aparecida Vilaça (personal communication 1/7/06) notes that a woman's lovers usually do not observe couvade. She adds that

> if the child gets sick and the [mother's husband] is observing tabus, [people reach] the conclusion that the mother had a lover. But she will deny it. Lovers are not accepted [as proper], though they exist.

William Crocker (2002, 89) gives us a remarkable account of pair bond/offspring notions among the Canela:

> [I]f a Canela's body has become polluted, these pollutants are necessarily passed to his or her closest kin—parents, siblings . . . , and children. This is because all these one-kin-link-away relatives . . . are believed to have almost identical blood . . . , so that all their blood is shared, as if they all lived in one blood pool . . . Grandparents, grandchildren, maternal uncles, paternal aunts, and cross-sibling nieces and nephews, being two kin-links from the fetus, have sufficiently dissimilar blood so that only nondamaging amounts of pollutants are passed on to them through the one intervening kinsperson.

Similarly, the Apinayé have a subclass of "true relatives," within which they further distinguish "birth relatives," also called "relatives whose blood is near" (Da Matta 1979, 89). "These persons are invariably members of the nuclear family of origin and/or marriage of the informants . . ." (*ibid.*). Kin-class relationships with such individuals, unlike those with all others, are not subject to tactical manipulation (Da Matta 1979, 90). This last fact has also been reported for the Araweté (Viveiros de Castro 1992, 160).

For the Kayapó, Fisher (2003, 126) reports a remarkable negative emphasis on primary kin relationships during certain rituals:

> During naming ceremonies, relations within the household and the nuclear family are displaced, so that the domestic and nuclear family division of labor, which is the normal pattern of food and substance production, is "switched off." In the alternative form organized by ritual, food production and sharing that are normally based on nuclear family ties are recast . . . A basic rule is that one should not eat the [food] from one's own child's ceremony . . . [Parents] of the ceremonially honored child should also not use their own or anybody else's earth oven for the duration of the ceremony. Ovens are associated with domestic residence . . . [T]he parental ban on the use of ovens also extends to eating together with one's own children or parents. Moreover, if the child's father is successful in procuring game during this period he must 'send it elsewhere' rather than consume it within the nuclear family. During the ceremonial period, nuclear family relations of the honored child should observe food restrictions . . . as if the child were sick and the group of [shared] substance at risk.

Moreover, "those mourning the death of a member of their immediate family (for example, a spouse, sibling, or child) have their hair cut short" (Turner 1980, 117). Turner (*ibid.*) expands on this as follows:

> Parents are thought to be connected to their children, and siblings to one another, by a tie that goes deeper than a mere social or emotional bond. The tie is imagined as a sort of spiritual continuation of the common physical substance that they share through conception . . . Although spouses lack the intrinsic biological link of blood relations, their sexual relationship constitutes a . . . libidinal community that is its counterpart. In as much as both sorts of biological relationship are cut off by death, cutting off the hair, conceived as the extension of the biological . . . self, is the symbolically appropriate response to the death of a spouse as well as a child.

Somewhat comparable is the Ache practice of local cannibalism, wherein the corpse may not be eaten by any of his/her primary kin (Clastres 1974, 314). A perhaps more tender expression of affection has been noted by W.H. Crocker (2002, 94) for the Canela. Here girls are encouraged by secondary kin to have ceremonial group sex, but their parents "were too embarrassed and too hindered by feelings to do this." Most poetic of all are Kracke's observations on food taboos in Kawahiv couvade ideology. Certain species are not consumed because they

> mark the additional responsibility undertaken in parenthood: cracids are notably monogamous birds in which both parents care for the young; and the curassaw is distinguished among the cracids by its elaborate courtship display, by the length of time the young are cared for by their parents, and by the vehemence with which the cock defends the nest . . . [Moreover, there are] the honeys forbidden for married people, [which], if eaten will harm the sexual partner (Kracke 1981, 131).

Chapter Eight

Evidence Re Sexual Jealousy

Beckerman *et al* (2002, 32) observe that, when Barí wives take lovers, "there is no evidence that the husbands objected." If this is true, the Barí are apparently unique in Amazonia. One of the commonest expressions of husbandly proprietorship and certainly the least acrimonious is the notion that extramarital affairs should be carried out at least with discretion or altogether surreptitiously. This is reported for the Canela (W. Crocker 1974, 195, 1984, 66; Crocker and Crocker 1994, 146–47), the Cashinahua (Kensinger 1984a, 244, 1984c, 2, 1995187–89; Lagrou 2000, 153), the Ese Eja (Peluso and Boster 2002, 144), the Kuikuru (Carneiro 1958, 138–39), the Mehinaku (Gregor 1973, 252–56, 1977, 293), the Tapirapé (Wagley 1977, 158), the Wari (Conklin 2001a, 119), and the Yanomami (Peters 1998, 118). Yet in some of these as well as other cases the cuckolded husband has been known to assault his wife and/or her paramour: this is reported for the Ache (Hill and Hurtado 1996, 443–44), the Araweté (Viveiros de Castro 1992, 164), the Cashinahua (Kensinger 1995, 187; Lagrou 2000, 154–55), the Guajá (Cormier 2003, 69), the Kawahiv (Kracke 1978, 28), the Kayapó (Bamberger 1979, 133), the Kuikuru (Carneiro 1958, 140), the Mehinaku (Gregor 1973, 247), the Tapirapé (Wagley 1977, 161), the Yanomami (Chagnon 1991, 147, 1997, 125; Peters 1998, 120–22), and the Yuquí (Stearman 1989, 95), and noted in a personal communication to me by Aparecida Vilaça for the Wari. Male sexual jealousy is recorded in myth for the Cashinahua (Lagrou 2000, 157), the Kawahiv (Kracke 1978, 24, 1981, 121), the Kayapó (William Fisher, personal communication), the Mehinaku (Gregor 1985, 30–31), and the Sharanahua (Siskind 1973, 104). In the last case it occurs in reality as well, though it seems to lead to nothing worse than quarreling (*ibid.*, 105). Watchful and suspicious husbands are reported for the Cashinahua (Lagrou 2000, 155) and the

Tapirapé (Wagley 1977, 141). In the latter case, shamanistic reprisal is directed at the cuckholder (*ibid.* 162). Among the Canela, marital infidelity sometimes leads to divorce (W. Crocker 1984, 66). To guard against it, a man who absents himself from his village may have his wife's behavior superintended by his or her parents (*ibid.*, 67). If his wife is nonetheless taken by another man he is likely to take revenge by having intercourse with the cuckholder's wife (*ibid.*, 88). Writing of a man whose wife was engaged in ritual dancing with other men, Crocker and Crocker (1994, 157) note that "he dashed out, consumed by jealousy, and grabbed his wife by the wrist, dragging her into the house to keep her for himself. Then he stood by the door and waved his machete in defiance of the men . . ." (see also W. Crocker 1974). And here are Heinen and Wilbert (2002, 215) on the Warao: "Warao men do not condone sexual relationships between their wives and other men. They are quite jealous of their spouses and demand the convocation of the assembly of villagers . . . to air and resolve cases of infidelity . . ." Finally, an email query to Terence Turner, asking if he had any evidence for sexual jealousy among the Kayapó, drew the single word reply, "Lots!" (personal communication 9/13/05).

Chapter Nine

Evidence Re the Denigration of Women

The best study of conceptualizations of sex and gender in Amazonia is Gregor (1985) on the Mehinaku, one of the populations with partible paternity. Each Mehinaku village contains a men's house, within which, as Gregor (*ibid.*, 92) notes

> . . . the men socialize, joke, and work on crafts. From its rafters hang the masks, costumes, and religious paraphernalia of the year's ritual calendar. But beyond these social and ceremonial functions, the men's house is the most visible symbol of the unity of the men and their opposition to the women. Any woman who enters the men's house, or who so much as glances at the sacred flutes stored inside, will be gang raped.

The flutes, according to myth, once belonged to women, from whom men stole them in the process of a general archetypical reversal of roles (*ibid.*, 112–14). This overall pattern—a men's cult in which sacred objects are manipulated and from which women are excluded by threat of force, plus "matriarchal" myths—is of course remarkably familiar from the ethnography of other areas, especially Papua New Guinea (Gregor and Tuzin 2001, Hays 1988; see also Gregor 1973, 1979, 1984, 1990).

Also reminiscent of Papua New Guinea are notions of feminine pollution.[1] Here is Gregor again (1985, 147):

> A recurrent theme in the Mehinaku culture of sexuality is that intercourse jeopardizes masculine identity. Full growth, a good stature, wrestling ability, and health all depend on restraint. Even when they are achieved, however, continued success may require sexual abstinence. Men's work roles are especially vulnerable to sexual activity. . . . [P]rior to a group fishing expedition, the villagers refrain from sexual relations since sex reduces the size of the catch. A woman

along on a major trip ensures its failure. . . . "Women's genitals," the men explain, "are revolting to the fish." Other work roles . . . such as housebuilding or monkey hunting, are also adversely affected by sex. A man who wants to be successful in his work does well to avoid excessive sexual contact with women (see also Gregor 1973, 243).

Something similar to the Mehinaku men's house, though apparently without "matriarchal" mythology, has been reported for the Bororo. Here women are forbidden, under penalty of death (Fabian 1992, 70), to see men impersonating spirits "associated with masculine vitality" (J. Crocker 1985, 105–06), to which boys are first exposed at puberty (*ibid.*, 106). These spirits find objective embodiment in bullroarers (*ibid.*), remarkably analogous to Mehinaku flutes.[2] Nor is this all. "A new mother, and a woman during her menses, contaminates all food and drink she contacts" (*ibid.*, 60). Her menses, at least, reflect "woman's essentially impure and corrupting nature (*ibid.*, 114).

In a personal communication, Terence Turner tells me that he found "matriarchy" myths among the Kayapó. Men's cults are not noted for the other populations under consideration, but notions of feminine pollution abound. These latter have also been noted for the Ache (Hill and Hurtado 1996, 233), the Apinayé (Da Matta 1982, 53), the Araweté (Viveiros de Castro 1992, 180), the Canela (Crocker and Crocker 1994, 147), the Cashinahua (Kensinger 1984c, 2, 1995, 60; McCallum 2001, 16), the Kawahiv (Kracke 1981, 98), the Kayapó (Fisher 2001, 128), the Sharanahua (Janet Siskind, personal communication), the Wari (Aparecida Vilaça, personal communication), the Yanomami (Peters 1998, 143), and the Yuquí (Stearman 1989, 88–89).

Only among the Ache are girls definitely reported to choose their own marital partners (Hill and Hurtado 1996, 227). By contrast, their marriages are arranged among the Canela (W. Crocker 1984, 65, 1990, 259; Crocker and Crocker 1994, 156), the Cashinahua (Kensinger 1995, 99, 2002, 20; McCallum 2001, 59), the Ese Eja (Peluso and Boster 2002, 139), the Guajá (Cormier 2003, 68), the Huaorani (Rival 1993, 641), the Kawahiv (Kracke 1978, 115–16, 1984, 108), the Kayapó (Lea 2002, 117), the Krahó (Melatti 1979, 69), the Kuikuru (Dole 1984, 51), the Kulina (Pollock 2002, 51), the Sharanahua (Siskind 1973, 79), the Warao (Suarez 1971, 92), the Wari (Conklin 2001a, 98), and the Yanomami (Àles 2000, 147; Chagnon 1988, 27, 1992, 6–8, 1997, 7; Peters 1998, 114).

The widespread existence of wife-beating and other forms of physical abuse against women among the populations under consideration has already been alluded to in connection with sexual jealousy and men's cult secrecy.

But it occurs for other reasons as well, as reported for the Cashinahua (Kensinger 1995, 187), the Kawahiv (Kracke 1978, 28), the Tapirapé (Wagley 1977, 161), and the Yanomami (Àles 2000, 149; Chagnon 1992, 147–49, 1997, 124–26; Peters 1998, 121). Gang rape has already been noted in connection with the Mehinaku men's cult. But it is also reported for the Canela (W. Crocker 1974, 187, 1984, 65; Crocker and Crocker 1994, 156), the Tapirapé (Wagley 1977, 159), and the Yanomami (Peters 1998, 117), and individual rape for the Mehinaku again in nonceremonial contexts (Gregor 1990, 485). In a personal communication dated 9/13/05, Terence Turner tells me that, among the Kayapó, "[t]here is ritual rape to assert male control over female sexuality and the fissive potential of male domestic family and household attachments, which may undermine the solidarity of men's communal groups."

Three ethnographers have provided us with general statements of male dominance among the populations under consideration. Here is W.H. Crocker (2002, 94) on the Canela:

> Men . . . marry across . . . the village circle. Living away from their wives, they nevertheless dominate their sister's households during most daily visits to them. . . . Through the [group of e]lders . . . , the men ran the society, keeping the political and ceremonial systems going and disciplining the young. In contrast, the women had no overarching institution similar to the [group of e]lders . . .

Gregor (1990, 484) summarizes the position of a Mehinaku woman as follows:

> From an early age she is told (mainly by men) that she is "just a girl." She is mainly fit to gossip, and in fact the term for a gossip of either sex is "woman mouth." She learns that her genitals are unattractive, and she is taught to comport herself modestly, so that no one will see her inner labia. If she is young and attractive, the men may shout aggressive remarks from the security of the men's house as she walks across the village plaza. At the time of her first menses she is secluded and takes medicines to staunch the flow of contaminating blood. Each month she must throw away food or water that the blood may have magically polluted. Men who are sick or ritually vulnerable will have to leave her house to avoid the contamination. A Mehinaku woman is therefore regarded as dangerous, sexually alluring, and yet at the same time, faintly ridiculous.

Peters (1998, 131–32) has this to say about the position of Yanomami women:

> Women are servants to men. Adult women serve their husbands and their children, especially their sons. Girls obey their fathers, mothers, and brothers. If a

child defecates, the men will turn their heads and voice their disgust. When a man discovers feces in the dwelling he will tell a woman to clean it up . . . [Moreover,] the reproductive activity of women holds little status or reward. With pregnancy a woman's fetus may be aborted, due to pressure from her husband or other women. At birth the female infant may be killed because of her sex, and if kept alive is referred to as a bitch. In childhood she is to replicate what Yanomami women do. She will soon participate in household chores such as baby-sitting, preparing food for the family, and accompanying her mother to the field . . . At this time males in the same age group are gleefully doing whatever they want to do. . . . [A] girl or woman has no say over whom she will marry. Her betrothal will be made on the basis of economic and social gain for the males of her family of origin. If she has been taken in a raid, she is likely to be gang-raped. . . . Bonds that she forms with other females, even sisters, are tentative . . . At the same time, men are free to form strong bonds . . . A wife is beaten by her husband for sexual [misbehavior]. She is to blame if she does not bear children and strongly criticized if she bears only females. Her primary life function terminates with the raising of her last infant. Her husband does not find it necessary to provide meat or protect her after she ceases bearing children. At death her body is placed in a shallow grave. . . . She is not warrior, hunter, or shaman, all of which are prestigious. She is considered incapable of surviving alone in the forest. She does not comprehend the full scope of the spirit world. . . . Should a male do some service generally done by women, like carrying water, he is mocked with . . . "You are a woman" . . .

Krahó women, Melatti (1979, 48) tells us plainly, "are totally excluded from political life."

NOTES

1. See Roscoe (2001) for a general statement (though focusing on Papua New Guinea) of the antipathy between sex and maleness.

2. Though less important than flutes, bullroarers are reported for the Mehinaku (Gregor 1984, 25, 1985, 105 *et seq.*). The widespread use of these latter has been noted by Dundes (1976), who, though remarking on their phallic character, emphasizes instead their significance in fantasies of anal birth. The Bororo expressly liken bullroarers to giant penises (J. Crocker *ibid.*). But see elsewhere (J. Crocker 1979, 294), where the spirit impersonators fling clay pellets at the women. The pellets "are explicitly said to represent the power of the male principle against the female" (*ibid.*).

Chapter Ten

Miscellaneous Evidence

The foregoing bodies of evidence can be supplemented in various ways. Thus, the claim that Amazonia is an erotic cornucopia is refuted not only by the copious evidence, noted above, for sexual jealousy and male fantasies about feminine pollution but also by other considerations which inhibit male sexual access to women. Thus, Hill and Kaplan (1988, 299) note that Ache "women who develop a reputation for engaging in extramarital sex may also have difficulty finding a new mate if they are abandoned by their spouse," and that some young men were discouraged by their parents from marrying or otherwise developing sexual relationships. "Their parents," they write, "forced them to sleep in the center of the camp where they could be observed easily, and during the day they were encouraged to hunt at the outmost periphery of the . . . band, most distant from the women . . . (*ibid.*, 301). Viveiros de Castro (1991, 189) reports that pre-pubescent Araweté girls are allowed considerable sexual freedom, but this is drastically curtailed by their parents and brothers. W.H. Crocker (1984, 72) makes much the same observation for the Canela. In the Araweté case, moreover, though women may have extramarital lovers, their sexual partners *en toto* should not exceed "two or three; more than this leads to a painful childbirth and splotchy skin . . ." (Viveiros de Castro 1992, 180). Similar magical notions of "too many fathers" are reported for the Kawahiv (Kracke 1981, 122), the Kayapó (Lea 2002, 106), the Mehinaku (Gregor 1973, 246, 1985, 89, 1990, 489), and the Tapirapé (Wagley 1977, 134), and related to me for the Huaorani by Laura Rival in a personal communication. Among the Bororo, according to J.C. Crocker (1985, 45), extramarital sex is considered morally wrong, and when it does occur all men who have had a hand in the production of a fetus are supposed to abstain from sex — not only with the mother but with all women — for a prolonged period during gestation and after birth, lest the fetus or infant be injured (*ibid.*, 49). Gregor (1977, 271) notes a comparable restriction on the sexual activity of the mother's husband among the Mehinaku. Beckerman and his associates report that most Barí women take lovers only after they are already pregnant (Beckerman *et al* 2002, 32)—something apparently true as well for the Tapirapé (Wagley 1977, 139). In other cases multiple paternity, though recognized as a possibility, is frowned upon: this is so for the Apinayé (Da Matta 1982, 50), the Ese Eja (Peluso and Boster 2002, 145–46), and the Yukpa (Halbmayer 2004, 148). This in turn strongly suggests the notion that sex should be restricted to a married couple—something expressly noted for the Apinayé (Da Matta 1982, 50), the Cashinahua (McCallum 2001, 61),[1] the Huaorani (Rival 1998, 620), and the Yuquí (Stearman 1989, 90). The Kawahiv go this one better, marrying a girl as soon as she reaches puberty, lest her children be regarded as illegitimate (Kracke 1978, 24). There is apparently such a concern that, in one case noted by Kracke (1984, 112), a girl was beaten by her brother to coerce her into early marriage. Writing of the Krahó, Melatti (1979, 90) notes that when a man goes on a journey, "his wife moves into the house of her parents-in-law, who watch over her to see that she does not have sexual relations with other men during the absence of her husband." Among the Ese Eja, "a child without a [co-resident] father is considered a disgrace . . ." (Lepri 2005, 715). Finally, there is this from Gregor (1985, 50) on the Mehinaku:

> Despite the villagers['] toleration of premarital sex, pregnancy out of wedlock is wrong. The . . . "mother of the illegitimate child" . . . is an object of scorn. The "fatherless child" is himself subject to abuse. As a result, most girls are married as soon as they emerge from the period of adolescent seclusion that follows their first menses.

Such restrictions on a woman's sexual freedom imply a considerable male concern with paternal certainty, for which there is some direct evidence. Here are Peluso and Boster (2002, 143) on the Ese Eja:

> The partible paternity of a child is [one] reason for giving it up for adoption. The smaller the proportion of paternity attributed to the mother's husband, the greater the chance that the child will be given up. In one community, 14 of the 27 children reported to have secondary fathers were given up for adoption, while only 6 of 46 children without secondary fathers were given up (52% vs. 13%; $X2 = 12.9$, $p<0.001$). Some mother's husbands insist on strict exclusivity. For instance, one girl explained why she is the only one of her parents' eight children that was not adopted out. "I am the only one who is purely [my father's], the rest are mixed. He didn't want to raise the others." Other cases verge on infanticide.

Comparable evidence can be found for the Ache (Hill and Kaplan 1988, 299), the Canela (W. Crocker 2002, 99), and the Warao (Heinen and Wilbert 2002, 215; see also Erikson 2002, 133–34 for other pertinent references.)

Similarly, Thomas Gregor informs me, in a personal communication dated 7/29/05, that, among the Mehinaku, a "mother who has a child resembling a man other than her husband has some explaining to do, and the child may even be at risk, very much like a stepchild." Writing of the Ache, Hill and Hurtado (1996, 274) report that, outside of marriage, "men sometimes preferred to deny paternal responsibility." Consistent with this are the attenuated couvade interdictions imposed upon a woman's sexual partners other than her husband: these are noted for the Canela (W. Crocker, 1990, 297–99), the Kulina (Pollock 2002, 55), the Mehinaku (Gregor 1985, 88), and the Wari (Conklin 2001a, 118).

There are reports of an emphasis on marital stability, especially when dependent children are involved. Significant here are the Canela (W. Crocker 1984, 88–89, 1990, 261–64; Crocker and Crocker 1994, 156; Nimuendajú 1946, 131), and the Cashinahua (McCallum 2001, 63). Correspondingly, the importance of extramarital affairs is sometimes minimized. Thus Vilaça (2002, 356) reports that they are "rarely admitted" among the Wari. Among the Cashinahua, according to Kensinger (1984a, 247), they "carry with them no long-term responsibilities." The Kayapó, Lea (2002, 106) tells us, "recognize the possibility of an individual having two or more genitors, but in practice it is uncommon." The same is true for the Apinayé (Da Matta 1982, 50).

NOTE

1. Kensinger (1984a, 244) reports that a woman may have lovers, but her husband has prior claim to her sexuality.

Chapter Eleven

Conclusion

It can now better be seen what partible paternity is *not*. It is *not* "group marriage": husbands are likely fathers and are virtually invariably distinguished from a woman's paramours or a mother's lovers. Related to this, in not a single case is there any report that a man has *full* brideservice obligations to the parents of his paramour, and only the Mehinaku have him "accept *some* of the obligations of in-laws when the child grows up and gets married" (Gregor, 1985, 88; emphases added). This is especially pertinent, for it is just what J.C. Crocker (1969) stressed in debunking another relatively recent attempt to find "group marriage" in Amazonia.

Nor does partible paternity signal a communal Eden in which a man gladly lends his wife to another man's pleasure, or where he regards women as his equal, or where he treats all children as well as he treats his own, or where our species' propensity to form pair bonds does not exist. Which is to say, of course, that *it is a variant of the human condition*, of what can be seen in "the West" and almost everywhere else. That it has been represented otherwise is a product of a sophomoric grasp of anthropological and especially kinship theory by Beckerman and Valentine, of Sarah Hrdy's venturing far beyond her professional competence, and of some cavalier science journalism on the part of Meredith Small.

What, then, *is* partible paternity — i.e. what regular behavior in addition to sexual variety does it entail? The answer, noted above by Beckerman and Valentine, is *provisioning* with meat from the hunt and/or fish from the catch. This is reported in the majority of cases — specifically, for the Ache (Hill and Hurtado 1996, 442–43), the Araweté (Viveiros de Castro 1992, 62), the Barí (Beckerman *et al* 2002, 33), the Canela (W. Crocker 2002, 102), the Cashinahua (Kensinger 1984a, 243, 1995, 10, 2002, 18 *et seq.*), the Ese Eja

(Peluso and Boster 2002, 138), the Matis (Erikson 2002, 134), the Mehinaku (Gregor 1973, 245, 1977, 146), the Sharanahua (Siskind 1973, 234), the Warao (Heinen and Wilbert 2002, 220), the Yanomami (Peters 1998, 119), and the Yuquí (Stearman 1989, 95). In addition, Loretta Cormier and William Fisher, in personal communications to me, note it for the Guajá and the Kayapó, respectively. With all this in mind, I submit that only the most naïve anthropologist would wish to make the case that the exchange of sex for provisions exists in Amazonia but not in situations one might wish to call "Western."

I have attempted here to disengage partible paternity from the mix of exoticism and essentialism that Beckerman and Valentine have put it in. It is neither very foreign to ideas closer to home nor is there a shred of evidence that it antedates them. Claims to the contrary constitute yet another primitivist project and have nothing at all to do with empirical inquiry.

Bibliography

Adams, William Y. 1998. The philosophical roots of anthropology. Stanford: CSLI
  Publications.
Àles, Catherine. 2000. Anger as a marker of love: the ethic of conviviality among the
  Yanomami. In the anthropology of love and anger: the aesthetics of conviviality in
  native Amazonia. Joanna Overing and Allan Passes, eds. London: Routledge. Pp.
  133–51.
———. 2002. A story of unspontaneous generation: Yanomami male coprocreation
  and the theory of substances. In Beckerman and Valentine 2002a. Pp. 62–85.
Bamberger, Joan. 1979. Exit and voice in Central Brazil: the politics of flight in
  Kayapó society. In Maybury-Lewis 1979. Pp. 130–46.
Barnard, Alan. 1978. Universal systems of kin categorization. African Studies
  37:69–81.
Basso, Ellen B. 1973. The Kalapalo Indians of Central Brazil. New York: Holt, Rine-
  hart and Winston.
Beckerman, Stephen, Roberto Lizarralde, Carol Ballew, Sissel Schroeder, Christina
  Fingelton, Angel Garrison, and Helen Smith. 1998. The Barí partible paternity proj-
  ect: preliminary results. Current Anthropology 39:164–67.
Beckerman, Stephen, Roberto Lizarralde, Manuel Lizarralde, Jie Bai, Carol Ballew,
  Sissel Schroeder, Dina Dajani, Lisa Walkup, Mayhsin Hsiung, Nikole Rawlins, and
  Michelle Palermo. 2002. The Barí partible paternity project, Phase One. In Beck-
  erman and Valentine 2002a. Pp. 14–26.
Beckerman, Stephen, and Paul Valentine. 2002a. Cultures of multiple fathers: the theory and practice of partible paternity in Lowland South America. Gainesville: University Press of Florida.
———. 2002b. Introduction: the concept of partible paternity among native South
  Americans. In Beckerman and Valentine 2002b. Pp. 1–13.
Besnier, Niko. 1994. Polynesian gender liminality through time and space. In Third
  sex, third gender: beyond sexual dimorphism in culture and history. Gilbert Herdt,
  ed. Pp. 285–328. New York: Zone Books.

Blackwood, Evelyn. 1997. Native American genders and spiritualities: beyond anthropological models and misrepresentations. In Jacobs *et al* 1997. Pp. 284–94.

Brumann, Christoph. 2000. 'Philoprogenitiveness' through the cracks: on the re-
silience and benefits of kinship in utopian communes. In Dividends of kinship:
meanings and uses of social relatedness. Peter P. Schweitzer, ed. Pp. 177–206. London: Routledge.

Burch, Ernest S., Jr. 1975. Eskimo kinsmen: changing family relationships in northwest Alaska. St. Paul, MN: West Publishing.

Cachel, Susan M. n.d. Using sexual dimorphism and development to reconstruct mating systems: another look. Unpublished ms.

Callender, Charles, and Lee M. Kochems. 1983. The North American 'berdache.'
Current Anthropology 24:443–70.

Carneiro, Robert L. 1958. Extra-marital sex freedom among the Kuikuru Indians of
Mato Grosso. Revista do Museu Paulista 10:135–42.

———. n.d. The concept of multiple paternity among the Kuikuru: a step toward the
new study of ethnoembryology. Unpublished ms.

Chagnon, Napoleon A. 1988. Male Yanomamo manipulations of kinship classifica-
tion of female kin for reproductive advantage. In Human reproductive behavior: a
Darwinian perspective. Laura Betzig, Monique B. Mulder, and Paul Turke, eds.
Cambridge: Cambridge University Press. Pp. 23–48.

———. 1992. Yanomamo: the last days of Eden. New York: Harcourt Brace & Company.

———. 1997. Yanomamo (5th edition). New York: Harcourt Brace & Company.

Chernela, Janet M. 1984. Female scarcity, gender ideology, and sexual politics in the
Northwest Amazon. In Kensinger 1984d. Pp. 28–36.

———. 1985. The sibling relationship among the Uanano of the Northwest Amazon:
the case of Nicho. In The sibling relationship in lowland South America. Kenneth
M. Kensinger, ed. Working Papers on South American Indians, Bennington College. Pp. 33–40.

———. 1993. The Wanano Indians of the Brazilian Amazon: a sense of space. Austin:
The University of Texas Press.

———. 2002. Fathering in the Northwest Amazon of Brazil: competition, monopoly,
and partition. In Beckerman and Valentine 2002a. Pp. 160–77.

Clastres, Pierre. 1974. Guayaki cannibalism. In Native South Americans: ethnology
of the least known continent. Patricia J. Lyon, ed. Boston: Little, Brown and Company. Pp. 309–21.

Conklin, Beth A. 2001a. Consuming grief: compassionate cannibalism in an Amazonian society. Austin: The University of Texas Press.

———. 2001b. Woman's blood, warrior's blood, and the conquest of vitality in Amazonia. In Gregor and Tuzin 2001. Pp. 141–74

———. 2002. "Thus are our bodies, thus was our custom": mortuary cannibalism in
an Amazonian society. In Ritual and belief: readings in the anthropology of religion. David Hicks, ed. Boston: McGraw-Hill. Pp. 210–35.

Cormier, Loretta A. 2003. Kinship with monkeys: the Guajá foragers of eastern Amazonia. New York: Columbia University Press.

Crocker, J. Christopher. 1969. Men's house associates among the Eastern Bororo. Southwestern Journal of Anthropology 25:236–60.

———. 1979. Selves and alters among the Eastern Bororo. In Maybury-Lewis 1979. Pp. 249–300.

———. 1985. Vital souls: Bororo cosmology, natural symbolism, and shamanism. Tucson: The University of Arizona Press.

Crocker, William H. 1974. Extramarital sexual practices of the Ramkokamekra-Canela Indians: an analysis of socio-cultural factors. In Native South Americans: ethnology of the least known continent. Patricia J. Lyon, ed. Boston: Little, Brown and Company. Pp. 184–94.

———. 1979. Canela kinship and the question of matrilineality. In Margolis and Carter 1979. Pp. 225–49.

———. 1984. Canela marriage: factors in change. In Kensinger 1984b. Pp. 63–98.

———. 1990. The Canela (Eastern Timbira): an ethnographic introduction. Washington: Smithsonian Institution Press.

———. 2002. Canela "other fathers": partible paternity and its changing practices. In Beckerman and Valentine 2002a. Pp. 86–104.

———. and Jean Crocker. 1994. The Canela: bonding through kinship, ritual, and sex. New York: Harcourt Brace.

Cromwell, Jason. 1997. Traditions of gender diversity and sexualities: a female-to-male transgendered perspective. In Jacobs *et al* 1997. Pp. 119–42.

Dabbs, James M. 2000. Heroes, rogues, and lovers: testosterone and behavior. New York: McGraw-Hill.

Daly, Martin, and Margo Wilson. 1988. Homicide. New York: Aldine de Gruyter.

Da Matta, Roberto. 1973. A reconsideration of Apinayé social morphology. In Peoples and cultures of native South America. Daniel R. Gross, ed. New York: The Natural History Press. Pp. 277–91.

———. 1979. The Apinayé relationship system: terminology and ideology. In Maybury-Lewis 1979. Pp. 83–127.

———. 1982. A divided world: Apinayé social structure. Cambridge, Mass.: Harvard University Press.

D'Andrade, Roy G. 1995. The development of cognitive anthropology. Cambridge: Cambridge University Press.

Dole, Gertrude E. 1969. Generation kinship nomenclature as an adaptation to endogamy. Southwestern Journal of Anthropology 25:105–23.

———. 1984. The structure of Kuikuru marriage. In Kensinger 1984b. Pp. 45–62.

Dundes, Alan. 1976. A psychoanalytic study of the bullroarer. Man 11:220–38.

Engels, Frederick. 1975 [1884]. The origin of the family, private property, and the state in the light of the researches of Lewis H. Morgan. New York: International Publishers.

Epple, Carolyn. 1997. A Navajo worldview and *nádleehí*: implications for Western categories. In Jacobs *et al* 1997. Pp. 174–91.

Erikson, Philippe. 2002. Several fathers in one's cap: polyandrous conception among the Panoan Matis (Amazonas, Brazil). In Beckerman and Valentine 2002a. Pp. 123–36.

Fabian, Stephen M. 1992. Space-Time of the Bororo of Brazil. Gainesville: University Press of Florida.

Fisher, William H. 1998. The teleology of kinship and village formation: community, ideal and practice among the Northern Gê of Central Brazil. In Unsettled communities: changing perspectives on South American indigenous settlements. Debra Picchi, ed. South American Indian Studies, Bennington College. Pp. 52–59.

——. 2001. Age-based genders among the Kayapó. In Gender in Melanesia and Amazonia: an exploration of the comparative method. Thomas A. Gregor and Donald Tuzin, eds. Berkeley: University of California Press. Pp. 115–40.

——. 2003. Name rituals and acts of feeling among the Kayapó (M?bengokre). The Journal of the Royal Anthropological Institute 9:117–35.

Fishman, Joshua A. 1960. A systematization of the Whorfian hypothesis. Behavior Science 5:323–39.

Flanagan, Cara. 1999. Early socialization: sociability and attachment. London: Routledge.

Fock, Niels. 1963. South American birth customs in theory and practice. In Crosscultural approaches: readings in comparative research. Clellan S. Ford, ed. New Haven: HRAF Press. Pp. 126–44.

Fortes, Meyer. 1953. The structure of unilineal descent groups. American Anthropologist 55:17–41.

Geertz, Clifford. 1983. Local knowledge: further essays in interpretive anthropology. New York: Basic Books.

Gottlieb, Alma. 2004. The afterlife is where we come from: the culture of infancy in West Africa. Chicago: The University of Chicago Press.

Gregor, Thomas A. 1973. Privacy and extramarital affairs in a tropical forest community. In Peoples and cultures of native South America. Daniel R. Gross, ed. New York: The Natural History Press. Pp. 242–60.

——. 1974. Publicity, privacy, and Mehinaku marriage. Ethnology 13:333–49.

——. 1977. Mehinaku: the drama of daily life in a Brazilian Indian village. Chicago: the University of Chicago Press.

——. 1979. Secrets, exclusion, and the dramatization of men's roles. In Margolis and Carter 1979. Pp. 250–69.

——. 1984. A Mehinaku myth of matriarchy. In Kensinger 1984d. Pp. 24–27.

——. 1985. Anxious pleasures: the sexual lives of an Amazonian people. Chicago: The University of Chicago Press.

——. 1990. Male dominance and sexual coercion. In Cultural psychology: essays on comparative human development. James W. Stigler, Richard A. Shweder, and Gilbert Herdt, eds. Cambridge: Cambridge University Press. Pp. 477–95.

——, and Donald Tuzin, eds. 2001. Gender in Amazonia and Melanesia: an exploration of the comparative method. Berkeley: University of California Press.

Gross, Paul R., and Norman Levitt. 1994. Higher superstition: the academic left and its quarrels with science. Baltimore: The Johns Hopkins University Press.

Guemple, Lee. 1972. Kinship and alliance in Belcher Island Eskimo society. In Alliance in Eskimo society. Lee Guemple, ed. Seattle: American Ethnological Society. Pp. 56–78.

Halbmayer, Ernst. 2004. "The one who feeds has the rights": adoption and fostering of kin, affines, and enemies among the Yukpa and other Carib-speaking Indians of lowland South America. In Cross-cultural approaches to adoption. Fiona Bowie, ed. London: Routledge. Pp. 145–64.

Hays, Terence. 1988. 'Myths of matriarchy' and the sacred flute complex of the Papua New Guinea highlands. In Myths of matriarchy reconsidered. Deborah Gewertz, ed. Sydney: University of Sydney. Pp. 98–120.

Heinen, H. Dieter. 1972. Economic factors in marriage alliance and kinship system among the Winikina-Warao. Antropologica 32:28–67.

——— and Werner Wilbert. 2002. Paternal uncertainty and ritual kinship among the Warao. In Beckerman and Valentine 2002a. Pp. 210–20.

Herdt, Gilbert. 1994. Introduction: third sexes and third genders. In Third sex, third gender: beyond sexual dimorphism in culture and history. Gilbert Herdt, ed. New York: Zone Books. Pp. 21–81.

Hill, Kim, and Magdalena Hurtado. 1996. Ache life history: the ecology and demography of a foraging people. New York: Aldine de Gruyter.

Hill, Kim, and Hillard Kaplan. 1988. Tradeoffs in male and female reproductive strategies among the Ache. In Human reproductive behavior: a Darwinian perspective. Laura Betzig, Monique B. Mulder, and Paul Turke, eds. Cambridge: Cambridge University Press. Pp. 277–305.

Hill. W.W. 1935. The status of the hermaphrodite and transvestite in Navaho culture. American Anthropologist 37:273–79.

Holmberg, Allan R. 1969. Nomads of the long bow: the Siriono of eastern Bolivia. New York: The Natural History Press.

Hrdy, Sarah B. 1999. Mother Nature: a history of mothers, infants, and natural selection. New York: Pantheon Books.

———. 2001. Mothers and others—co-operative breeding. Natural History, May issue.

Jacobs, Sue-Ellen, Wesley Thomas, and Sabine Lang, eds. 1997. Two-spirit people: Native American gender identity, sexuality, and spirituality. Urbana: University of Illinois Press.

Jankowiak, William R., and Laura Mixson. 2008. "I have his heart, swinging is just sex": ritualization of sex and the rejuvenation of the love bond in an American spouse exchange community. In Intimacies: love and sex across cultures. William R. Jankowiak, ed. New York: Columbia University Press. Pp. 245–65.

Jay, Nancy. 1985. Sacrifice as remedy for having been born of woman. In Immaculate and powerful: the female in sacred image and social reality. Clarissa Atkinson, Constance H. Buchanan, and Margaret R. Miles, eds. Boston: Beacon Press. Pp. 283–309.

———. 1992. Throughout your generations forever: sacrifice, religion, and paternity. Chicago: The University of Chicago Press.

Keesing, Roger M. 1975. Kin groups and social structure. New York: Holt, Rinehart and Winston.

Kensinger, Kenneth, M. 1984a. An emic model of Cashinahua marriage. In Kensinger 1984b. Pp. 22–51.

———. 1984b (ed.). Marriage practices in lowland South America. Urbana: University of Illinois Press.

———. 1984c. Sex and food: reciprocity in Cashinahua society. In Kensinger 1984d. Pp. 1–3.

———. 1984d (ed.). Sexual ideologies in lowland South America. Working Papers on South American Indians, Bennington College.

———. 1995. How real people ought to live: the Cashinahua of eastern Peru. Prospect Heights: Waveland Press.

———. 2002. The dilemmas of co-paternity in Cashinahua society. In Beckerman and Valentine 2002a. Pp. 14–26.

Konner, Melvin. 1990. Why the reckless survive and other secrets of human nature. New York: Viking.

Kracke, Waud H. 1978. Force and persuasion: leadership in an Amazonian society. Chicago: The University of Chicago Press.

———. 1981. Don't let the piranha bite your liver: a psychoanalytic approach to Kagwahiv (Tupi) food taboos. In Food taboos in lowland South America. Kenneth M. Kensinger and Waud H. Kracke, eds. Working papers on South American Indians, Bennington College. Pp. 91–142.

———. 1984. Kagwahiv moieties: form without function? In Kensinger 1984b. Pp. 45–62.

Kronenfeld, David B. 1996. Plastic glasses and church fathers: semantic extension from the ethnoscience tradition. Oxford: Oxford University Press.

Lagrou, Elsje M. 2000. Homesickness and the Cashinahua self: a reflection on the embodied condition of relatedness. In The anthropology of love and anger: the aesthetics of conviviality in native South America. Joanna Overing and Alan Passes, eds. London: Routledge. Pp. 152–69.

Lakoff, George. 1987. Women, fire, and dangerous things: what categories reveal about the mind. Chicago: The University of Chicago Press.

Lang, Sabine. 1997. Various kinds of two-spirit people: gender variance and homosexuality in Native American communities. In Jacobs *et al* 1997. Pp. 100–18.

———. 1998. Men as women, women as men: changing gender in Native American cultures. Austin: The University of Texas Press.

Lea, Vanessa. 1995. The houses of the M?bengokre (Kayapó) of Central Brazil—a new door to their social organization. In About the house: Lévi –Strauss and beyond. Janet Carsten and Stephen Hugh-Jones, eds. Cambridge: Cambridge University Press. Pp. 206–225.

———. 2002. Multiple paternity among the M?bengokre (Kayapó, Jê) of Central Brazil. In Beckerman and Valentine 2002a. Pp. 105–22.

Lee, Richard B. 1968. What hunters do for a living, or, how to make out on scarce resources. In Lee and DeVore 1968. Pp. 30–48.

———. 1979. The !Kung San: men, women, and work in a foraging society. Cambridge: Cambridge University Press.

———. 1988. Reflections on primitive communism. In Hunters and gatherers: history, evolution, and social change. Tim Ingold, David Riches, and James Woodburn, eds. Oxford: Berg. Pp. 252–68.

———. 1992. Art, science, or politics? The crisis in hunter-gatherer studies. American Anthropologist 94:31–54.

———, and Richard Daly. 1987. Man's domination and woman's oppression: the question of origins. In Beyond patriarchy: essays by men on pleasure, power, and change. Michael Kaufman, ed. Toronto: Oxford University Press. Pp. 30–44.

———, and Irven DeVore. 1968. Man the hunter. Chicago: Aldine.

Lehrman, Daniel S. 1970. Semantic and conceptual issues in the nature-nurture problem. In Development and evolution of behavior: essays in memory of T.C. Schneirla. Lester R. Aronson, Ethel Tobach, Daniel S. Lehrman, and Jay S. Rosenblatt, eds. San Francisco: W.H. Freeman and Company. Pp. 17–52.

Lepri, Isabella. 2005. The meanings of kinship among the Ese Eja of northern Bolivia. The Journal of the Royal Anthropological Institute 11:703–24.

Levine, Nancy E. 1988. The dynamics of polyandry: kinship, domesticity, and population on the Tibetan border. Chicago: The University of Chicago Press.

Loizos, Peter, and Patrick Heady. 1999. Introduction. In Conceiving persons: ethnographies of procreation, fertility, and growth. Peter Loizos and Patrick Heady, eds. London: The Athlone Press. Pp. 1–17.

Lounsbury, Floyd, G. 1964. A formal account of the Crow- and Omaha-type kinship terminologies. In Explorations in cultural anthropology: essays in honor of George Peter Murdock. Ward H. Goodenough, ed. New York: McGraw-Hill. Pp. 351–93.

———. 1969. The structural analysis of kinship semantics. In Kinship and social organization. Paul Bohannon and John Middleton, eds. New York: The Natural History Press. Pp. 125–48.

Lowie, Robert H. 1920. Primitive society. New York: Boni & Liveright.

Malinowski, Bronislaw. 1913 [1963]. The family among the Australian aborigines. New York: Schocken Books.

Margolis, Maxine L., and William E. Carter, eds. 1979. Brazil: anthropological perspectives. New York: Columbia University Press.

Marshall, Lorna. 1976. The !Kung of Nyae Nyae. Cambridge, Mass.: Harvard University Press.

Maybury-Lewis, David H.P., ed. 1979. Dialectical societies of the Gê and Bororo of Central Brazil. Cambridge, Mass.: Harvard University Press.

McCallum, Cecelia. 2001. Gender and sociality in Amazonia: how real people are made. Oxford: Berg.

Melatti, Julio C. 1979. The relationship system of the Krahó. In Maybury-Lewis 1979. Pp. 46–79.

Morgan, Lewis H. 1871. Systems of consanguinity and affinity of the human family. Washington: Smithsonian Institution.

——. 1877. Ancient society, or researches in the lines of human progress from savagery through barbarism to civilization. New York: Henry Holt and Company.

Munn, Nancy O. 1970. The transformation of subjects into objects in Walbiri and Pitjantjatjara myth. In Australian Aboriginal anthropology: modern studies in the social anthropology of the Australian aborigines. Ronald M. Berndt, ed. Nedlands: the University of Western Australia Press. Pp. 141–63.

Murdock, George P. 1947. Bifurcate merging: a test of five theories. American Anthropologist 49:59–60.

——. 1949. Social structure. New York: The Free Press.

——. 1957. World ethnographic sample American Anthropologist 59:664–87.

——. 1959. Cross language parallels in parental kin terms. Anthropological Linguistics 1:1–5.

Murphy, Robert F. 1979. Lineage and lineality in lowland South America. In Margolis and Carter, 1979. Pp. 217–24.

Nimuendajú, Curt. 1946. The Eastern Timbira. Berkeley: University of California Press.

Overing Kaplan, Joanna. 1975. The Piaroa, a people of the Orinoco Basin: a study in kinship and marriage. Oxford: Clarendon Press.

Oyama, Susan. 1985. The ontogeny of information: developmental systems and evolution. Durham: Duke University Press.

Parkin, Robert. 1997. Kinship: an introduction to the basic concepts.

——, and Linda Stone, eds. 2004. Kinship and family: an anthropological reader. Oxford: Blackwell.

Peletz, Michael G. 1995. Kinship studies in late twentieth century anthropology. Annual Review of Anthropology 24:343–72.

Peluso, Daniela M., and James S. Boster. 2002. Partible parentage and social networks among the Ese Eja. In Beckerman and Valentine 2002a. Pp. 123–59.

Peters, John F. 1998. Life among the Yanomami. Peterborough, Canada: Broadview Press.

Peterson, Nicolas. 1997. Demand sharing: sociobiology and the pressure for generosity among foragers. In Scholar and sceptic: Australian Aboriginal studies in honour of L.R. Hiatt. Francesca Merlan, John Morton, and Alan Rumsey, eds. Canberra: Aboriginal Studies Press. Pp. 171–90.

Pilling, Arnold R. 1997. Cross-dressing and shamanism among selected western North American tribes. In Jacobs *et al* 1997. Pp. 69–99.

Pinker, Steven. 1997. How the mind works. New York: W.W. Norton & Company.

——. 2002. The blank slate: the modern denial of human nature. New York: Viking Books.

Pollock, Donald. 2002. Partible paternity and multiple maternity among the Kulina. In Beckerman and Valentine 2002a. Pp. 42–61.

Prince Peter of Greece and Denmark. 1963. A study of polyandry. The Hague: Mouton.

Ramos, Alcida R., and Bruce Albert. 1976. Yanoama descent and affinity: the Sanuma/Yanomam contrast. Actes du 42nd Congres International des Americanistes Vol. II. Pp. 71–90.

Rival, Laura M. 1993. The growth of family trees: understanding Huaorani perceptions of the forest. Man 28:635–52.

———. 1998. Androgynous parents and guest children: the Huaorani couvade. The Journal of the Royal Anthropological Institute 4:619–42.

———. 2002. Trekking through history: the Huaorani of Amazonian Ecuador. New York: Columbia University Press.

Rivière, Peter G. 1969. The Trio: a principle of social organization. Oxford: Clarendon Press.

———. 1974. The couvade: a problem reborn. Man 9:423–35.

Roscoe, Paul. 2001. "Strength" and sexuality: sexual avoidance and masculinity in New Guinea and Amazonia. In Gregor and Tuzin 2001. Pp. 279–308.

Roscoe, Will. 1994. How to become a berdache: toward a unified analysis of gender diversity. In Third sex, third gender: beyond sexual dimorphism in culture and history. Gilbert Herdt, ed. New York: Zone Books. Pp. 329–72.

Sanday, Peggy R., 1986. Divine hunger: cannibalism as a cultural system. Cambridge: Cambridge University Press.

Scheffler, Harold W. 1973. Kinship, descent, and alliance. In Handbook of social and cultural anthropology. John J. Honigmann, ed. Chicago: Rand McNally. Pp. 747–93.

———. 1978. Australian kin classification. Cambridge: Cambridge University Press.

———. 1991. Sexism and naturalism in the study of kinship. In Gender at the crossroads of knowledge: feminist anthropology in the postmodern era. Micaela di Leonardo, ed. Berkeley: University of California Press. Pp. 361–82.

———, and Floyd G. Lounsbury. 1971. A study in structural semantics: the Siriono kinship system. Englewood Cliffs, NJ: Prentice-Hall.

Scheper-Hughes, Nancy. 1992. Death without weeping: the violence of everyday life in Brazil. Berkeley: University of California Press.

Schneider, David M. 1984. A critique of the study of kinship. Ann Arbor: The University of Michigan Press.

Seeger, Anthony. 1981. Nature and society in Central Brazil: the Suya Indians of Mato Grosso. Cambridge, Mass.: Harvard University Press.

Shapiro, Judith. 1968. Tapirapé kinship. Boletim do Museu Paraense Emilio Goeldi 17:1–32.

———. 1984. Marriage rules, marriage exchange, and the definition of marriage in lowland South American societies. In Kensinger 1984b. Pp. 1–30.

Shapiro, Warren. 1973. Residential grouping in northeast Arnhem Land. Man 89:365–83.

———. 1979. Social organization in Aboriginal Australia. Canberra: The Australian National University Press.

———. 1981. Miwuyt marriage: the cultural anthropology of affinity in northeast Arnhem Land. Philadelphia: Institute for the Study of Human Issues.

———. 1988. Ritual kinship, ritual incorporation, and the denial of death. Man 23:375–97.

———. 1990. Of 'origins and essences': Aboriginal conception ideology and anthropological conceptions of Aboriginal local organization. In On the generation and maintenance of the person: essays in honour of John Barnes. Warren Shapiro, ed. Sydney: The University of Sydney Press. Pp. 208–21.

——. 1995. Fuzziness, structure-dependency, and 'structural anthropology': an extended reply to Parkin. Journal of the Anthropological Society of Oxford 26:197–214.

——. 1996. The quest for purity in anthropological inquiry. In Denying biology: essays on gender and pseudo-procreation. Warren Shapiro and Uli Linke, eds. Lanham, MD: University Press of America. Pp. 167–89.

——. 1998. Ideology, 'history of religions,' and hunter-gatherer studies. The Journal of the Royal Anthropological Institute 4:489–510.

——. 2003. Review of Harold W. Scheffler, Filiation and affiliation, and Richard Feinberg and Martin Oppenheimer, eds. The cultural analysis of kinship: the legacy of David M. Schneider. American Anthropologist 105:375–77.

——. 2005. Universal systems of kin categorization as primitive projects. Anthropological Forum 15:45–59.

Silk, Joan B. 1987. Adoption and fosterage in human societies: adaptations or enigmas? Cultural Anthropology 2:39–49.

Siskind, Janet. 1973. To hunt in the morning. Oxford: Oxford University Press.

Small, Meredith F. 2003. How many fathers are best for a child? Discover Magazine.

Spiro, Melford E. 1986. Cultural relativism and the future of anthropology. Cultural Anthropology 1:259–86.

Stanner, W.E.H. 1960. On Aboriginal religion: II: sacramentalism, rite, and myth. Oceania 30:245–78.

Stearman, Allyn M. 1989. Yuquí: forest nomads in a changing world. New York: Holt, Rinehart and Winston.

Stocking, George, W., Jr. 1987. Victorian anthropology. New York: The Free Press.

Stone, Linda. 1987. Kinship and gender: an introduction. Boulder: Westview Press.

Suarez, Maria M. 1971. Terminology, alliance, and change in Warao society. Nieuw West-Indische Gids 48:56–122.

Thayer, James S. 1980. The berdache of the northern Plains: a socioreligious perspective. Journal of Anthropological Research 36:287–93.

Thomas, N.W. 1906. Kinship organizations and group marriage in Australia. Cambridge: Cambridge University Press.

Tiger, Lionel, and Joseph Shepher. 1975. Women of the kibbutz. New York: Harcourt Brace Jovanovich.

Tooker, Elizabeth. 1971. Clans and moieties in North America. Current Anthropology 12:357–76.

Turner, Terence S. 1979. Kinship, household, and community structure among the Kayapó. In Maybury-Lewis 1979. Pp. 179–214.

——. 1980. The social skin. In Not work alone: a cross-cultural view of activities superfluous to survival. Jeremy Cherfas and Roger Lewin, eds. Beverly Hills: Sage Publications. Pp. 112–40.

Valentine, Paul. 2002. Fathers that never exist: exclusion of the role of shared father among the Curripaco of the Northwest Amazon. In Beckerman and Valentine 2002a. Pp. 178–91.

Vilaça, Aparecida. 2002. Relations between funerary cannibalism and warfare cannibalism: the question of predation. Ethnos 65:83–106.
———. 2002. Making kin out of others in Amazonia. The Journal of the Royal Anthropological Institute 8:347–65.
Viveiros de Castro, Eduardo. 1992. From the enemy's point of view: humanity and di-
   vinity in an Amazonian society. Chicago: The University of Chicago Press.
Wallace, Ben J. 1969. Pagan Gaddang spouse exchange. Ethnology 8:183–88.

www.ingramcontent.com/pod-product-compliance
Lightning Source LLC
Chambersburg PA
CBHW030657270326
41929CB00007B/402